Jesus 2.1

An Upgrade for the 21st Century

Thomas W. Shepherd, D.Min.

ALSO BY THE AUTHOR

Good Questions
Answering Letters From the Edge of Doubt
(Unity House, 2009)

Friends in High Places
Tracing the Family Tree of New Thought Christianity
(Unity Books, 1985; revised 3rd Edition, iUniverse
Press, 2006)

Glimpses of Truth
*Systematic Theology From a Metaphysical Christian
Perspective*
(UFBL Press, 2000)

Science fiction written under the pen name
Thomas Henry Quell

The Princess and the Prophet
(iUniverse Press, 2003)

Wrathworld
(iUniverse Press, 2002)

Jesus 2.1

An Upgrade for the 21st Century

Thomas W. Shepherd, D.Min.

unity® HOUSE

Unity Village, MO 64065-0001

Jesus 2.1

First Edition

Unity House books are available at special discounts for bulk purchases for study groups, book clubs, sales promotions, book signings or fundraising. To place an order, call the Unity Customer Care Department at 1-800-251-3571 or e-mail *sales@unityonline.org.*

Bible quotations are from the New Revised Standard Version unless otherwise indicated.

Cover design: Doug Brown, Unity Multimedia Artist
Interior design: The Covington Group, Kansas City, Missouri

Library of Congress Control Number: 2010930989
ISBN: 978-0-87159-335-1
Canada BN 13252 0933 RT

For the Rev. Don Jennings,

Teacher, minister, friend—
who told me I was one with God,
and demonstrated by his life
how natural it is
to find the Imago Dei
in everyone.

"Well done, thou good and faithful servant, ... enter thou into the joy of thy Lord."—Matthew 25:21 (KJV)

Contents

Who Was Jesus?

Even his own publicists had different opinions of who Jesus of Nazareth was. The writer of the Gospel of Matthew came to the conclusion that he was indeed the Messiah of Israel, yet never quite explained what *Messiah* really meant. Was Jesus to be identified with the Cosmic Christ of the Gospel According to John, or the Suffering Son of God according to the writer of Mark? Or was he perhaps driven by the social agenda suggested by the Gospel of Luke?

Do we even know if the question "Who was Jesus?" would have made any sense to the writers of the Christian Scriptures? No wonder that so many people, in the 2,000 years since he walked the earth, have held differing opinions about him. For some people through the ages, Jesus was, and still is, in the words of the Nicene Creed,

> ... the Lord Jesus Christ, the only-begotten Son of God, begotten of the Father before all worlds, God of God, Light of Light, Very God of Very God, begotten, not made, being of one substance with the Father by whom all things were made.[1]

Others found this "One Solitary Life"[2] reflected what they wished their God to be. In 1740, Charles Wesley penned the song "Jesus Lover of My Soul" and the next year Handel's *Messiah* took the words from the Hebrew Bible and attributed to Jesus *Wonderful, Counselor, Prince of Peace*.[3] For multitudes of people— from the time of the writing of the Gospels to today—Jesus of

Nazareth has become the Christ, a process that has been many things to many people. To some, Jesus has been a source of comfort, to others a Savior, and to still others the Way Shower, and many more things than any one can imagine. Throughout history countless people from a wide variety of theological perspectives have been able to say with deep conviction, "He walks with me."

In this collection of Christological essays, the Rev. Dr. Thomas Shepherd, my friend and Unity Institute colleague, has suggested there must be an evolutionary component in any understanding of the Man of Nazareth. I am hopeful that Shepherd's efforts to place Christology in an evolutionary context will help individuals to see that any understanding of the man Jesus—who revealed God so completely that he continues to be called *the Christ*—must continue to evolve. This work can also help people understand that, while believers continue to attribute to Jesus an amazing array of titles, it is terribly important for progressive thinkers to understand the most important term of all. Shepherd contends that the Christ, as applied to the historical Jesus, applies equally to all humanity today.

If Jesus walks with me, I can be more tolerant of others, whether they feel his presence or not. If everyone is made in the *Imago Dei*, all have the same Christ-within, even while treading divergent paths and walking hand-in-hand with a different Christ.

Evelyn J. Niles
Unity Institute

All hail the power of Jesus' Name!
Let angels prostrate fall;
Bring forth the royal diadem,
And crown Him Lord of all.
Bring forth the royal diadem,
And crown Him Lord of all.

—"All Hail the Power of Jesus' Name,"
Edward Perronet (1726–1792)

And He walks with me,
And He talks with me,
And He tells me I am His own;
And the joy we share as we tarry there,
None other has ever known.

—"In the Garden," C. Austin Miles (1868–1946)

What if God was one of us?
Just a slob like one of us,
Just a stranger on the bus
Trying to find his way home ...

—"One of Us," Eric Bazilian (1953–)

Preface

Caveat Lector

(Latin, *"Let the reader beware"*)

This book presents one theologian's point of view at this slice of the timeline. The opinions expressed herein are not necessarily the final word on Christology for the author, let alone any organized religious institution, denomination or school of theology. Expect many good questions and very few eternal answers.

Some Acknowledgements

I owe the impetus for writing this volume to the Rev. Dr. Mary Tumpkin, president of the Universal Foundation for Better Living (UFBL). For about 15 months I worked as assistant executive director of that organization, which was founded by the charismatic leader Rev. Dr. Johnnie Colemon. When Dr. Tumpkin asked me to work on a volume about Christology, little did I imagine the task would stretch over 10 years and become one of the central studies of my professional life. I began researching this book while working as a denominational official for the UFBL in the summer of 2000, continued the project after accepting the pastorate of Sunrise Unity Church, Sacramento, California, and finally completed the work in the spring of 2010, while serving in my current position as chair of the Historical and Theological Studies department at Unity Institute, Unity Village, Missouri.

I want to thank my lovely wife, Carol-Jean, for diligently scrubbing the manuscript, checking biblical quotes (I'd messed up a few), and generally elbowing me in the eye when I got too verbose or pedantic. I also want to acknowledge the work of my Unity Institute colleague, Rev. Evelyn J. Niles, who read the final draft and made several critical suggestions that have been incorporated in the present volume. In fact, I would be remiss if I did not thank all my present and former teachers, fellow students, colleagues and co-workers at Lancaster School of Theology, Iliff School of Theology, Saint Paul School of Theology, Unity Institute, the Unitarian Universalist Association, the Universal Foundation for Better Living, the Unity School of Christianity, and Unity Worldwide Ministries (formerly the Association of Unity Churches International). While all of the above helped to make this book possible, let me formally absolve them of any culpability in its sometimes heretical conclusions.

Let me add a personal testimonial. Although this book deconstructs—i.e., takes a solid whack at—more than a few human concepts of Jesus handed down through history, throughout my life I have never ceased to be a Jesus person. Even while attempting to topple the culturally biased, often bigoted, images by which some of his friends have tried to characterize the man behind the myth, Jesus has always been special to me. It is from this position of reverence, love and respect that the book you are about to read proceeds.

Finally, let me reiterate what I have said about all my work: this book does *not* represent the official theology of any organization, publishing house, church body or theological institution. This is one theologian's musing about the most important figure in Western history. You are invited to join the ongoing Christological discussion. This is a book about a work in progress, i.e., remaking and reprogramming the ancient images for the world in which you live. Therefore, I cordially invite you to begin downloading this *Jesus 2.1* upgrade, realizing you may have to rewrite the program to fit the unique circumstances of your life, where God is doubtless working through your consciousness to bring forth the highest, greatest good.

Introduction

> The fact that astronomies change while the stars
> abide is a true analogy of every realm of human
> life and thought, religion not least of all. No exis-
> tent theology can be a final formulation of spiri-
> tual truth.[1]
>
> —Harry Emerson Fosdick,
> *The Living of These Days*

Why add to the towering pile of books about Jesus of
Nazareth? One might reasonably argue that too much has already
been written about him. What possible good can another volume
of Jesus-talk do in today's postmodern, post-9/11, post-Christian
world? Surely all the great ideas about the man from Galilee have
already fought their way into print. What fair wind of change
could another discourse on Christology—by yet another self-
appointed theologian—add to the hurricane of words blowing
through Christendom for the past 2,000 years?[2] People have continued to eat, drink, marry and give in marriage, and they have
muddled through quite nicely without the current volume to
guide them. Isn't it obvious that, while making their lives
and raising their families, people have successfully managed
to make and remake Jesus Christ based on the needs of each successive era?

Yet it is just that observation—the successive remaking of
Jesus, vertically through history and horizontally through contemporary cultures—which distinguishes this book from other
works of Christology. *Jesus 2.1: An Upgrade for the 21st Century*
takes seriously the creative process by which people have shaped

their Jesuses. In fact, I will argue that creative interaction with inherited images and ideas about Jesus constitutes a healthy, positive course of intellectual and spiritual growth, an essential component in any understanding of Jesus Christ and the faith bearing his name.

There is nothing particularly innovative about the observation that thought-pictures of Jesus have been repainted through time. Authors like Albert Schweitzer and Jaroslav Pelikan have detailed the history of Christological metamorphosis. Schweitzer said the process was unavoidable; Christology must be progressive.

> Each successive epoch found its own thoughts in
> Jesus, which was, indeed, the only way in which
> it could make him live ... one created him in
> accordance with one's own character.[3]

Rather than lament the lack of a clear-cut, authentic, historical Jesus from whom to receive perfect guidance, this volume celebrates the ongoing process of Jesus-building, choosing instead to see the culturally influenced images of the Christ as an attempt to get a better look at the *Imago Dei*, the image of God inscribed within each individual. The central point this book attempts to make is that the flexibility of a progressive Christology allows each new generation to discover more about their true nature by discovering themselves in Jesus the Christ.

Furthermore, the discussion proceeds from a postmodern premise, i.e., not only are there multiple paths to the same truth, but also multiple truths accessible along a dizzying diversity of paths. Not just the blind men and a lone elephant; other creatures, great and small, stand unidentified in the fuzzy dawn of a new, quantum universe. Reputable scientists now suspect that human thought has the power to shape reality in a way that probably would have scared Sir Isaac Newton out of his powdered wig.

Taking the multiplicity of truth as a given, the long history of Christological interpretation and reinterpretation becomes much easier to understand. Harry Emerson Fosdick, one of the great preachers of the 20th century, advocated openness to new thoughts as a survival tactic for any religious system.

> If the day ever comes when men care so little for the basic Christian experiences and revelations of truth that they cease trying to rethink them in more adequate terms, see them in the light of freshly acquired knowledge, and interpret them anew for new days, then Christianity will be finished.[4]

To be fair to Fosdick's vision, he was a modernist, not a postmodernist, in that he believed there was only one truth and the goal was to refine one's thinking to grow ever closer to this singular view of reality. He also lived in a time before women rightly raised awareness about the need for inclusive language when speaking of humanity at large. Postmodernists, as mentioned above, postulate an amazing array of "truths" that individuals can comprehend, none of which may be singularly correct for all persons at all times. It is precisely this kind of open-ended discussion that can inform the search for new understandings of Jesus Christ for today and into the future.

Humanity has consistently and creatively recreated the son of Joseph and Mary to meet the needs of each new age. Most recent books written about the changing images of Jesus through time have attempted to recover the original person buried under all the modifications. Some have felt the historical Jesus enjoys special authority, or at the very least a unique and authoritative voice. Consequently, the closer we come to what he actually said and did, the closer we move to The Truth. This book sets off in a different direction. Acknowledging that people remake Jesus in each generation, I will argue, as Schweitzer did, that without a progressive Christology, the richness of the Jesus Event will be frozen in time, trivialized and ultimately lost. As Schweitzer also noted, it is probably impossible to reconstruct the historical Jesus from the documentary evidence, the best of which comes from biased sources who were not themselves eyewitnesses.

Now you have a thumbnail sketch of the book's central thesis, but this work is less a systematic argument than a collection of ideas. Essentially, the current work is a series of essays to introduce a new application of an old, old story—a Jesus Christ upgraded for the 21st century. In the following chapters, you will participate in the celebration of a Jesus for *now*, taking for granted that all Jesuses for the future and all historical Jesuses from the past are, and should be, products of different needs.

Toggling the Image of God

To continue playing with the computer metaphor, let's imagine that the *Jesus 2.1* upgrade will reinstall the Jesus Christ operating system and quarantine any lingering remnants of culturally induced viruses that may have contaminated earlier versions (e.g., Jesus as the blonde European crusader with a penchant for burning witches), then install a revised *Imago Dei*, which some users have cross-referenced with the eternal Christ. Once installed in your thinking, *Jesus 2.1* should make it easier to toggle the image of God among all sentient beings. This internal-eternal Christ can be discovered in the historical-biblical Jesus, but all interaction with Jesus comes through dialogue with models that have been shaped and reshaped through time and can be accessed through historical-critical study, some of which is included in the bundled *Jesus 2.1* software.

Jesus is arguably both a point of reference and a meeting place for discussion of values, like a program that has been adapted through the ages while the basic code remains undisturbed despite all subsequent modifications. Now it is our time to rewrite and reinstall the Jesus program with updates for today, just as every previous generation has done and every subsequent generation will do.

The Romans killed Jesus for being a revolutionary. Every succeeding generation kills him anew by losing sight of the ongoing revolution in human consciousness that he represents. The idea is both simple and sublime—God within humanity, *Imago Dei*, becomes flesh and dwells among us, and everything we have said about this long-dead Galilean can be said about every human being who evolved on this glorious, violent, beautiful little planet.

The Kingdom of God will never come from the skies with fire and judgment, but perhaps we can build a democratic model of God's Commonwealth instead. Starting with the ongoing task of finding new ways to love each other, we can work to end war and poverty, bring health and prosperity to everyone, and go forward to the stars as one people united. Then we shall see what other mysteries have been revealed in the cosmos by the outpicturing divine creativity as the sacred process of life continues.

Jesus calls people to follow him because he knows where the path leads. When and if the call reaches ready minds and hearts, like the fishermen long ago, people silently leave their nets of complacency and begin the journey anew.

First Thoughts

Theological reflection is a subversive activity; it makes people uncomfortable; it will make you uncomfortable. This is to be expected; the discomfort is a sign that you are breaking chains that bind you, that you are investigating new lands, that you are taking greater control over your life. It is your opportunity to distinguish the God who has called you from all other gods (and there are many!) and, like Joshua, commit yourself and your congregants to serving and worship the One God.[1]

—Rev. Dr. Robert Martin

New Heavens, Many Earths, New Hermeneutic

We live in an age when, almost daily, astronomers are discovering extrasolar planets that orbit nearby stars. This cornucopia of new worlds suggests the tantalizing, wildly optimistic possibility of a *Star Trek* future when it might be commonplace for humans to fly to earth-type alien worlds on the wings of technologies yet unborn.

Here on earth more readily achievable biotech advances offer the alluring possibilities of an end to disease, vastly increased human intelligence and stamina, and even physical immortality—or at least Methuselan longevity. Yet the spoiling specters of environmental disaster and rampant global terrorism haunt the sacred paths of science. Science alone is not a guarantor of a benevolent future world. Historians and theologians have noted that fascist Germany sprouted from a highly educated, sophisticated society; Hitler coldly adjusted that skill base to his own nefarious devices. The brain trust employed by the Nazis fervently researched the sciences, invented modern rocketry, and produced detailed biotech plans to improve its "racial stock" through eugenics and euthanasia. Germanic Christianity—incontestably the lighthouse of Protestant thought in the early 20th century—could not guide its people through the dark sea of fascism, nor could its great theological and ethical lights prevent the massive cultural shipwreck of the Holocaust.

In a contemporary milieu fraught with tendencies toward sadism and self-destruction, yet offering the potential for unbounded opportunities, perhaps an enhanced understanding of Christology is more important than ever. The model of humanity presented in that "one solitary life" arguably has the potential to counterbalance all the Hitlers and Stalins humanity ever produced.[2] Jesus Christ is such an influential figure in human history that a new vision of who he was, how he has changed through time, and what he continues to be in human consciousness might be indispensable for a postmodern, high-tech, galaxy-facing culture.

"Take me to your Savior ..."

If a team of visiting scholars from another solar system decided to look into the central figure in Christianity, they would quickly discover a baffling array of Jesuses offered by an equally bewildering marketplace of "Christian" groups. Digging into the piles of Jesus profiles, they might conclude there is no central organizing principle that unites the disparate Jesus images. Christian loyalties notwithstanding, we must allow that the alien researchers would have a point. Place the suffering, redeeming Jesus of Roman Catholicism beside the sin-busting Jesus of American fundamentalism; invite into the circle the mystical Jesus of Quaker spirituality, the status-quo-shaking Jesus of feminist theology, and the patriotic-triumphant Jesus of Mormonism. Call a suburban Protestant Jesus to the group, then add the provocative Jesus of New Testament scholarship and the prophetic Jesus of black liberation theology. For good measure, drop a Muslim Jesus into the mix (he's an Islamic prophet, you know). The visiting off-worlders might glance at each other and mumble, "This is not the same specimen of *Homo sapiens*."

But of course he is. There was only one historic Jesus. The problem is that Jesus models have never coincided, not even during his earthly ministry. The inherited biblical Jesuses are inconsistent to the point of contradiction. Mark's Jesus is too human, John's too divine. This confusion is one of many reasons why people seldom go to the Bible to get religious ideas; people are more likely to read the Bible with religious ideas already decided. Wearing the lenses of their embedded theologies, people look to the Scripture for validation and emotional support. Roman Catholics who read the Bible will not encounter the same Jesus as Mormons or Quakers. It could scarcely be otherwise.

Although common sense suggests human thought starts somewhere, the indisputable fact is that all ideas are shaped by what has happened to us in the past. Even the most objective scholar begins by putting on a lens that induces her to conclude, "Objective thinking works best here ..." Human belief systems hardly function by pure logic based on total objectivity; in fact there is no vantage point from which we can look down upon life and arrive at an unbiased opinion. We approach all decisions with a set of preferences we did not specifically choose yet are operational nonetheless. To examine the nature of embedded beliefs, I need only remind myself that if complete impartiality were possible, everyone reading this book would root for the Philadelphia Phillies and prefer onion bagels to wheat toast, just like me.

Even while acknowledging to the panel of scholarly aliens that we are unable to divest ourselves completely of embedded assumptions about Jesus, we must also confess that the Man of Nazareth is irreplaceable in human consciousness. Whether looking at 21st-century life in terms of science or spirituality, politics or philosophy, economics or ethics, mental health or matters of the heart, Jesus continues to play an essential role in the collective consciousness of Western civilization.

Even those who grew up in Christian lands only to reject Jesus utterly, often for good reasons, have usually rejected Jesus because of values inherited *from* Jesus. For example, those who renounce Jesus because they find the "One Way" language of American fundamentalism intolerant and mean-spirited have unconsciously affirmed the tolerance and inclusive spirit that the biblical Jesus showed to all people, even the hated Romans. It usually isn't Jesus who turns people off—it's some of his small-minded friends.

Jesus is too important to dismiss due to the overzealous proclamations of his self-appointed spokespersons. Because of the continued importance of Europe and the Americas in world political, cultural and economic spheres, some degree of Christological reflection is important for humanity at large, whether Christian or not. The same could be said of Muhammad, whose 1.5 billion adherents form the second largest religious family on earth. In fact, I would argue that college students everywhere could profit from a reasonably objective, self-consciously unbiased, nondogmatic study of the world religions, including the foundational prophets and foremost thinkers of each major faith. My students in world religions at Unity Institute have insisted that the best part of the course was hearing from guest speakers who represented groups we had studied, which provided opportunity for Q&A and widened our outlook of a faith community previously represented by text and lecture alone.

Studying the Jesus Event today requires a fresh perspective, because most people have heard too much about Jesus to know anything about him. The older Jesus program was installed on the hard drives of modern minds through childhood religious education and perpetuated by a conservative Christian media that refuses to let humanity come of age. However, unlike my guest speakers from world religions, it is not possible to invite the historic Jesus to speak today as a corrective measure to this earlier programming. Meditatively, perhaps, one can have a one-to-one with Jesus that could be quite informative. But unless one's operating system is updated with new input, the chances are that any Jesus encountered through meditative experiences will sound remarkably like the "greatest hits" of the older Jesus model.

What is possible is to re-examine the recorded memories and interpretative history standing behind the Jesus programs already running in human minds, then download an update based on insights from postmodern biblical studies and theology. New clarity can be achieved after reconfiguring thought by rebooting it through a new application of Christology. As this process begins, the older version will be easily recognized as obsolete, unable to interface with the circumstances of postmodern life. It does not require a full diagnostic sweep of the Christian faith to recognize that humanity needs an updated Jesus program.

Consequently, this book will attempt to provide that kind of biblical-theological update, offering new input by which people can reinstall and restart their faith in the greatest life ever lived. Representing more than 10 years' work, the book is an attempt to pull together some of my theological reflections, essays, ruminations and stray thoughts on the most-written-about and least-agreed-upon figure in world history. Certainly, Jesus Christ needs no introduction. He is the ultimate incumbent, holding office for 2,000 years in Western consciousness.

Yet despite how all people *feel* about Jesus, very little is actually known about him historically, and the scant historical information has only recently begun to be discussed in language that can be understood by nonprofessionals. Books by scholars like Karen Armstrong, Marcus J. Borg, John Dominic Crossan, Bart Ehrman, Robert W. Funk, John Shelby Spong and others have begun to bridge the divide between theological scholarship and popular awareness, but there is still much work to be done. Historian and biblical scholar Elaine Pagels writes:

> What I've learned through studying the Gospel of Thomas and the context of the politics of early Christianity is that anyone who participates in Christian tradition without having learned anything about it—and that's most people who participate in it, because it's not taught in public or private schools for the most part—often think of their traditions as immutable, as if they've just come down from God.[3]

Although not everyone realizes it, a host of delightful, ongoing controversies present themselves in Christian thought, idea-rich disagreements that provide various ways to look at Jesus the Christ. This volume attempts to chart some of the most delicious disputes, and in so doing encourage readers to rethink, reshape and reinvent the Jesus paradigm for today. Plato said that an unexamined life is not worth living, and one could easily convert that old maxim into a Christological formulation: No matter how passionately a believer loves him, an unexamined Christology is not worthy of Jesus.

Because of this strangely uninformed familiarity about Jesus Christ, it will be necessary to offer a few words of introduction about the most-discussed life ever lived. The discussion begins with two hidden assumptions about Christology.

Two Hidden Assumptions

> Dr. Karl Barth was one of the most brilliant and complex intellectuals of the twentieth century. He wrote volume after massive volume on the meaning of life and faith. A reporter once asked Dr. Barth if he could summarize what he had said in all those volumes. Dr. Barth thought for a moment and then said: "Jesus loves me, this I know, for the Bible tells me so."[4]

Neo-orthodox theologian Karl Barth was known for his sophisticated ideas, yet this German-speaking professor chose a children's hymn to express the deepest sentiments of his thought. The uncomplicated language of this Sunday school song masks a deep well of meaning. Its plain verse inadvertently describes a complexity beyond any straightforward identification with Divine compassion, otherwise Barth never would have chosen it as an example of his system. "Jesus loves me" can be seen as a confident assertion of a one-on-one relationship with the Supreme Power in the Universe, a source of identity that describes the circle of faith. Likely it is this sense that Barth wanted to invoke by choosing the hymn.

Despite the clean lines of thought behind Barth's musical selection to illustrate his theology, clarity and objectivity in looking at Jesus are often difficult to achieve. For example, notwithstanding its simplicity and apparent inclusiveness, there is a narrower way to interpret the "Jesus Loves Me" lyrics. Two hidden assumptions, embedded within the belief systems of many Christians today, can be distilled from the lovely words that generations of believers have learned to sing as children.

1) Jesus is on my side ("Jesus loves me, this I know")

Unfortunately, some followers of Jesus are so heavily invested in the authority of the man from Galilee that they feel an almost frantic need for vindication through his words and deeds, so that the affection they believe Jesus bears for them—and they reciprocate for him—somehow legitimizes their belief systems.

If Jesus loves me, surely he stands with me. If Jesus stands with me, his footprints in my camp validate my belief system and my moral and political values. The approval of Jesus means I hold the proper Christian position on public health care policy, taxation, abortion, gay rights and gun control. If Jesus stands on the other side of any of these issues— well, he simply can't stand on the other side, because he is always right. And since I am on the right side, Jesus must be here too.

A full-blown hermeneutical system—i.e., a network of interpretative principles that inform biblical analysis—can be derived from a hidden assumption that Jesus *must* be on my side ("Jesus loves me, this I know"). Such a hermeneutic draws energy from the strong need to agree with Jesus, or better still to have Jesus agree with me. Its belief formula looks like this:

I know what is right.
Jesus is always right.
Therefore, Jesus must agree with me.
I receive my marching orders from the Bible.
Obedience is the goal for the Christian.

2) The Bible is literally true ("For the Bible tells me so")

The conclusion that God is on my side requires believers to nourish a second hidden assumption, i.e., the Bible is a coherent, harmonious document that supports my belief system ("For the Bible tells me so"). To follow such a naive, unbiblical prescription requires reinterpretation of problem passages until the offending texts conform to one's ethics and theology. Any hint of discord, any disturbing instance where Jesus does something that is less than admirable—cursing a fig tree not in season or promising to send violent judgment rather than peace upon the earth—forces true believers to rescue the text with creative interpretation to assuage their cognitive dissonance. For literalists who hold that Jesus is perfect, infallible and uniquely divine, the best which can be hoped for is blissful ignorance of this dynamic at work, because willfully deconstructing the authority of Jesus would pull the theological foundation from underfoot and rip the ceiling off the universe of biblical literalism.

Karl Barth never would have gone there. He was too faithful to Jesus to let biblical inerrancy be the *sine qua non* of Christian faith.[5]

Cafeteria Christianity: "Pick and Choose"

This assumption of total harmony is not restricted to evangelicals; progressives and even flat-out liberals often rush to the Scripture to validate their ethical and theological positions. Some Christian thinkers seem to cringe at the notion of interpretative authority resting solely within the individual interpreter. When we lived in Georgia, we sometimes attended worship services conducted by a now-retired mainline clergyman, a deeply spiritual gentleman whom I greatly admired. Although he was an outstanding preacher and pastor, he nevertheless considered the tendency to "pick and choose" among biblical ideas to be a shocking rejection of biblical faith. A popular term for this is *Cafeteria Christianity*, a derogatory label for Christians who

> ... pick and choose what doctrines they want to follow and what doctrines they want to ignore. ... They believe that they do not have to follow the rules of anyone. They are in charge and they can believe what they want.[6]

Whenever I have heard this argument, I've found myself muttering, "Of course people pick and choose!" Christianity is definitely a cafeteria, not a hot dog stand. The faith of Jesus is a smorgasbord of possibilities, better still, it's a supermarket where the believer can select from a wide variety of spiritual foods, take them home, and cook up endlessly different, deliciously individualized servings of spiritual sustenance. A Christian faith with many choices is not only possible; it is demanded by faith and reason. Everyone picks and chooses, and not only in their religious thinking. Whether reading the newspaper or pouring over Scripture, voting for a political candidate or exploring religious faith, people exercise their God-given power of judgment to select wholesome spiritual fare.

Sometimes I think the argument against so-called Cafeteria Christianity sounds like parents fretting after they have shouted to misbehaving children, "Because I said so!" Yes, there are times when adults have to look a kid in the eye and say, "Nice try. Now, eat your vegetables, clear the table, and put your coat on, it's freezing outside." Most children eventually grow up and learn which of their parents' eternal verities have any staying power in the next generation.

They pick and choose.

My unscientific suspicion is that many self-described Christians handle conflicts between problematic biblical texts and everyday reality by selectively perceiving those ideas that work for them and setting up firewalls within the canon of Scripture to protect themselves from cognitive dissonance. These artificial walls nevertheless shape the individual's cosmos and provide a frame of reference by which everything is evaluated. Yet there is a better way, which keeps the psyche undivided and the believer grounded in life's experiences.

Truth Self-Validates

Rather than assuming Jesus is a perfect, infallible source of divine revelation and the Bible speaks with one voice, this book accepts another formula, one that is followed by most biblical scholars today. The "new" approach? Simply this: *Let the Bible be what it is, ancient spiritual literature written by human beings.* This alternative point of view is hardly a radical innovation for 21st-century readers, although it differs profoundly from the earlier, revelation-based hermeneutic, which relied upon external authority. Truth validates itself by demonstrating its value rather than demanding a religious pledge of allegiance.

Pushing beyond theories of supernatural revelation, it becomes clear that the whole bundle of ideas, traditions and practices which comprise the Christian faith is a valiant, human attempt the carry divine truth in earthen vessels. Instead of bricking Jesus and the Second Testament authors into a temple of biblical perfection, let's consider the possibility that, although Jesus and the early Christian communities put forth an amazing array of great teachings, some of their ideas will not work today. Taking the discussion even further and crossing into what seems like new territory for Christian thought, let's step over the imaginary line that borders the sacred and secular worlds and propose that Jesus of Nazareth, like any great teacher, has no special authority whatsoever except when he says something that connects with the listener.

This requires postmodern thinking, which is not always a painless adjustment. Certainty is comfortable. Even if we dismiss a literal inerrancy of the biblical texts, shall we take the next step and question the authority of Jesus himself? Retired Episcopal Bishop John Shelby Spong remarks that the old idea of biblical authority dies hard:

> To face this reality is essential to my integrity as a Christian, but it is not easy. My religious critics say to me that there can be no Christianity apart from the authority of the scriptures. They hear my attack on this way of viewing the Bible as an attack on Christianity itself. I want to say in response that the claim that the scriptures are either divinely inspired or are the "Word of God" in any literal sense has been so destructive that I no longer want to be part of that kind of Christianity.[7]

Certainly, when people interact with the biblical sources they can learn and grow, but arguably neither the authority of Jesus nor the infallibility of the Bible is what stimulates growth. Women and men grow spiritually when seeds planted in their consciousness take root, expand, bloom and eventually produce what the apostle Paul called "fruit of the spirit."[8] In line with the above, let's consider a simplified hermeneutical statement that meets the tests of postmodern life:

I have values that are important to me.
Jesus and I do not always agree.
The Second Testament authors and I do not always agree.
When we dialogue, I learn.
Understanding is the goal.

Daunting Task

Jesus Christ through the centuries has been an extraordinarily fertile source of spiritual nourishment. Jesus has been studied, sermonized about, meditated upon, prayed to, worshiped and admired daily for 2,000 years. Yet his very familiarity makes it a daunting task to approach the Nazarene from any new direction. Like being raised with a kid brother, we know him too well to know anything about him. The charming childhood ditty that proclaims, "Yes, Jesus loves me," doesn't guarantee I am thinking clearly about Jesus. Or that Jesus and I always agree.

A balanced, prudent view of Jesus acknowledges that the historical Jesus is unavailable today except through the filters and lenses of Scripture, tradition, experience and reflection, and the product of this process comes with an expiration date stamped on the bottom. Jesus in the beginning decades of the 21st century is not likely to remain the same figure at the turn of the 22nd when our descendents reconstruct him. Both the historical Jesus and the manufactured, reinterpreted theological Jesus still have the power to speak meaningfully to humanity through the haze of changing times and cultures.

The "Christ of Faith"

If most Americans were shown a 30-something Caucasian man wearing a white robe, shoulder-length hair and close-cropped beard, chances are the identity-center of their brains would automatically chirp, "Yeah, I know that guy." Chances are the answer wouldn't be, "That's John Lennon!" The fair-skinned, robed image immediately conjures up memories of stained glass portraits and full-color prints of childhood, despite the fact that the Nazarene probably looked less like a Norse Viking and more like a Bedouin Arab. So why is this instant recognition software installed in almost everybody's brain? Because *they know him.*

Notwithstanding his long-ago lifetime and lofty location in literature and liturgy, Jesus for many people is not some distant deity, enthroned in Olympian splendor. Men and women today feel intimately acquainted with Jesus. People you and I have met and known personally insist that they have met and known Jesus, personally. People swear he has changed their lives, made them better human beings. Not only that, he continues to do so. He walks with them and talks with them—not in the distant past, but now, in the 21st century. Although no one alive today has stood face-to-face with the historic figure whose memory glows amid the shadows of antiquity, many people alive today really, really love Jesus in an intimate and personal way, like a loved one gone to war—distant, yet present in living memory, preserved by reread letters and daily conversations.

Removing or at least refocusing devotional lenses, the picture gets both clearer and more complicated. Some religious scholars argue that most Jesus concepts which have come down to us are actually based on a *Christ of faith*, a customized icon of Christian devotion, created and recreated in successive generations to meet the needs of the era.[9] These scholars are at least technically correct; it is an undisputed historical fact that people have reinterpreted and reshaped the image of Jesus, depending on where and when they lived. The ascetic Jesus of the third century is a wholly different spiritual being than the richly enthroned Jesus of late 16th-century Elizabethan Protestantism, and neither is recognizable in the revivalist Savior of the American frontier. Asian Christians tend to paint the Master with almond eyes. African Christians see him as black—which is probably an overstatement, but nevertheless stands closer to the Semitic original than the Scandinavian Jesus of European sacred art.

There is nothing particularly sinister about this; people reproduce themselves in their religious art because those are the available models. That which is normative is that which a person sees in daily life. Ordinarily, the innocuous act of creating the world in one's image proceeds unexamined, especially when it functions well. When applied to Jesus, the results of this image-building process are predictable.

Jesus Christ: Work-in-Progress

Albert Schweitzer—Nobel Peace Prize winner, gifted musician, selfless medical missionary, and accomplished biblical theologian—freely acknowledged the ongoing process of recreating Jesus. "Each successive epoch found its own thoughts in Jesus," Schweitzer wrote, "which was, indeed, the only way in which it could make him live."[10]

One might go further and also say, not without controversy, that the man of Nazareth has been an imaginary spiritual playmate for millions—best friend, confidante, silent lover, surrogate father-brother-husband; trusted King when earthly governments fail; all-purpose superhero who will save the day before the final credits roll. Sympathetic skeptics might say: "No matter. Love is always irrational. So long as the people who worship him are happy in their 'relationship' with the Jesus they have created, what's the difference?"

Any objective observer would have to agree, to a point. Dream-state spirituality based on a manufactured Christ of faith does not necessarily belie the reality of a connection to Jesus himself, because none but a cynic would deny that daily visits with the devotional Jesus have enriched countless lives. This acknowledgement requires any postmodern investigator to begin Christological study with a frank appreciation for the Christ of faith, regardless of how culturally bound the image may be. Billions of people who have worshiped Jesus as Master, Savior and Lord have incontestably entered into a faith-relationship with something beyond the reach of rational inquiry, a spiritual resource that puts them in touch with God and grants them assurance of pardon, strength for daily living, and peace of mind.

That being said, it should be briskly apparent that this book is not intended for the "Master-Savior-Lord" section of the Church Universal but for the skeptics and questioners in the crowd, the people who admire—perhaps even feel great affection for—Rabbi Yeshua Ben Josef, yet nevertheless want to climb beyond religious infatuation while firmly grasping the steady rail of contemporary thought during their ascent. My suspicion is their numbers are legion. During my 30-plus years in ministry, I have frequently encountered postmodern "believers" who hunger for the intimacy of personal belief but are not willing to surrender the head to gain the heart. Yet even these suspicious anti-traditionalists intuitively know that something is special about this man. His praise of the peacemakers, his love of truth, his blessing and approval of children, his stories that show acceptance of foreigners and outcasts, his willingness to speak to women as equals—these are extraordinary qualities that sparkle within the scriptural picture of Jesus.

One could argue that these traits appeal to modern readers primarily because life in the 21st century has shaped the way they look at social ethics, underscoring the conciliatory, compassionate elements in the Gospel narrative as both virtuous and definitive. Jesus today represents forgiveness, inclusivity and unconditional love. This sentimental description of Jesus as the God-man who loves and approves of everyone, the very incarnation of Beatle George Harrison's Hindu gospel song "My Sweet Lord," would be wholly unintelligible to large portions of the Christian world until the late 19th or early 20th centuries. In the past, Christians have invoked Jesus as a judge-executioner, god of war, avenging angel, and abusive father-figure meting out harsh discipline that today would be called child abuse. Historically, some Christians have seen a consistency between a judgmental God-as-Jesus and a judgmental God-as-Father/Creator. Although the Hebrew Scripture contains frequent references to God as merciful and steadfast in love, the overwhelming god-image that has persisted portrays YHWH of Sinai as the original abusive parent.

In 312 CE the first Christian Emperor said that God had instructed him to emblazon symbols of the Christ on the shields of his legions. When meeting his rival, Maxentius, at the Battle of the Milvian Bridge, Constantine apparently believed it was those symbols that bought him victory. This was not the Jesus of Martin Luther King Jr., but a Lord of battle who smote the foe in the Name of Almighty God. Medieval armies would march under the cross as they pillaged their way across Europe to rescue the Holy Land from the heathen Muslims, and the crimes committed along the way shamed the Christian faith and triggered a cry of anguish that is still heard today.

Not only have governments abused people in the name of Jesus. European children were taught by strict "Christian" standards, like the parents of the Protestant reformer Martin Luther, who beat him for minor offenses until the blood flowed. Until relatively recently, beggars and debtors were tossed in prison, women had no rights, and even the mildest offenses were met with death by hanging. Childhood had no meaning until the abolition of child labor, and African slavery made a mockery of the Sermon on the Plain with its *Blessed are the poor.* Only after humans had lived through these tough times did they begin to discover in the words of Jesus a better way to better living, a model hidden in his miracle stories and rabbinic instructions, perhaps waiting for humanity to mature unto the point when people understood that to love one another and love your enemies were not contradictory mandates.

Yet, as a template for human character, Jesus of Nazareth certainly offers a full array of healthy choices. He was a spiritual adventurer who forgave those who needed forgiveness, challenged those who needed a contradictory voice, and met people where they were. He grew, learned, loved, feared, conquered his fears, and remained faithful unto death. When it was all over, in the ebbing moments of his life, he prayed for forgiveness on behalf of the very people who had murdered him.

Would that all of us could go and do likewise.

Deep appreciation for the contributions of Jesus to human life—even love of Jesus, if you will—should not blind people to the facts about Jesus, or the lack thereof. Having made these preliminary remarks, which were designed to suggest the complexity and depth of the Jesus subject, let's take a deep breath, step back from the haze, and begin with some first thoughts about the most important person who ever lived.

An Ordinary Man Who Changed the World

No prophet goes through life unscathed.[1]
—Matthew Fox

Confessing the Obvious

Shall we begin by confessing the obvious? Jesus was a human male, a fully credentialed member of the species *Homo sapiens*. He was not born of the union between deity and virgin mother, because that's not how the natural order, which drives the biology of human beings, operates. Stories of supernatural origin were common in antiquity and survive in popular culture today. From Achilles and Alexander to Spiderman's accidental inheritance of superhuman powers from the bite of a mutant spider and Superman's extraterrestrial birth among the semidivine Kryptonians, people like their heroes extra-ordinary, licensed by the storyline to act extraordinary. Moved by life's tragedies yet never daunted; stirred, but not shaken.

Even so, only Matthew and Luke know anything of the virgin birth (*parthenogenesis* in Koine Greek), and a fresh reading of their nativity tales clearly shows the paraphernalia of mythology. Mark and John do not mention the birth of Jesus at all, nor does the earliest Second Testament writer, Paul, who certainly would have invoked parthenogenesis among his Greek congregations if he had any inkling the story were true.

Even the name attached to this towering, historical figure—
Jesus *Christ*, the term by which he is celebrated and wor-
shipped—is wrapped in misunderstanding. Biblical scholar and
Jesus Seminar founder Robert W. Funk observed:

> Many people today think there were a Joseph
> Christ and a Mary Christ to complete the holy
> family; Christ is actually a title, meaning the
> "anointed one" and is the Greek term that corre-
> sponds to the Hebrew title messiah.[2]

Apparently, young Jesus of Nazareth lived a rather ordinary
life as a member of his community. Despite valiant attempts to
create a backstory for the humble carpenter, there is no evidence
Jesus ever studied with the Essenes, Egyptians, Druids or Hindu
sages. Quite the contrary, he sounds very much like a first-
century rabbi, schooled in the prophetic tradition of Israel. He
apparently lived at home in Nazareth, where he learned and
grew, and when he reached early middle age (30-something), he
began to teach others his insights on the nature of God and the
meaning of life. He healed some people—more accurately, the
Gospels seem to suggest he summoned healing *from* them, often
remarking it was *their* faith that made them whole.

He conveyed his major teachings through storytelling, and his
parables and one-liners had a strongly ethical and universalist
flavor. When addressing the religious leaders of his day, he
employed the imagery of Jewish apocalyptic prophets to warn of
dire consequences that result from a life without faith and compassion. Although he repeatedly counseled against violent
responses to life's problems, Jesus was a spiritual revolutionary.
He was afraid of neither the Judean religious establishment nor
the might of Imperial Rome. Not surprisingly, he did not live long
enough to retire. As Matthew Fox observed, prophets seldom

amble through life untrammeled. Pastoral ministries specialist Jay Wells adds a biblical memory:

> Jesus faced opposition. In every crowd, someone questioned his motives and sought to discredit him. If it happened to him, it will happen to you.[3]

Unquestionably, he brought that opposition on himself. Jesus was an anachronism, a quixotic figure who roared onto the first-century scene as if he thought the age of prophecy was still in full bloom. If Jesus had stayed home in Nazareth and taught religious principles, or even if he had just wandered through the country-side preaching peace and love like the world's first hippie, his story might have ended differently. It certainly would have ended much later. Not content with operating at the fringe of society, Jesus took his prophetic challenge to the center of Jewish life and, like all great prophets before him, showed no inclination to compromise. You know the story.

Jesus visited the Jewish Temple during Passover week and criticized the economic and religious leadership in Jerusalem. The resulting tumult threatened public order. Roman authorities frankly could not have cared less what nonsense the Jews believed, but it had better not lead to trouble in the streets. Jesus' activities disrupted the Roman peace—one can almost hear Pilate's military advisers reporting, "This lunatic attacked the money changers and merchants in the Court of the Gentiles, by Jove!"

So the political leadership abruptly executed him as an insurrectionist. Jews get blamed for it, because the Christian community at the end of the first century was primarily non-Jewish and wanted to distinguish itself from the parent religion. By the time the Second Testament was written, Rome had fought a major war to put down a Jewish revolt, destroyed the Temple, and had begun expelling Jews from the imperial capital.

Certain enigmatic passages in the Second Testament—where Jesus is said to have been persecuted by "the Jews" and a Jewish crowd shouts for Pilate to execute a Jewish holy man and to free a criminal—make sense only in the above context, especially considering that both Jesus and all his followers seem to have been lifelong, faithful Jews. By the time the Gospels were written, Christians were not just willing to give excuses *for* the Romans, many Christians *were the Romans*. This pattern had already begun in the first generation. Paul, reportedly a citizen of Rome, taught the Gentiles they did not need to become full Jews to receive God's *Christos*. They were not under Law, but grace.

Nonetheless, it was the Romans who crucified him, not the Jews. After his execution, a significant number of people believed Jesus was still available to them in prayer, visions and inner communion. They carried his faith to all parts of the Roman world and eventually around the globe. Unfortunately, some who came later placed more emphasis on the messenger than the message he taught.

Son of the Great Gull?

If Jesus was fully human, which is a fair assumption considering he was born and died a man, and if there is any credibility to the legends about his great gifts of wisdom and healing power, one might deduce that all people have the potential to achieve similar insights, work similar wonders. If only a few individuals achieved this high level of consciousness (i.e., holiness) so far, some mystics have observed it may be due to inherited, limited ways of thinking rather than inherent limitations. It is, however, much easier to think of Jesus as extraordinarily abnormal—even uniquely divine—because his special qualities then provide an alibi for human limitations and justify human apathy in the face of a world filled with spiritual challenges.

In an extraordinary little volume, which set best-seller records in the young adulthood of the baby-boom generation, Richard Bach narrates a revelatory discussion between a flock of feathered disciples and the resurrected *Jonathan Livingston Seagull:*

> He spoke of very simple things—that it is right for a gull to fly, that freedom is the very nature of his being, that whatever stands against that freedom must be set aside, be it ritual or superstition or limitation in any form. ...
>
> "The only true law is that which leads to freedom," Jonathan said. "There is no other."
>
> "How do you expect us to fly as you fly?" came another voice (from the flock).
>
> "Look at Fletcher! Lowell! Charles-Roland! Judy Lee! Are they also special and gifted and divine? No more than you are, no more than I am. The only difference, the very only one, is that they have begun to understand what they really are and have begun to practice it."[4]

Love your enemies? Impossible! We're not Jesus. Just as the flock dismissed any hope of ever becoming equal to the "Son of the Great Gull,"[5] humans can linger safely in a comfort zone of mediocrity if convinced that higher achievement is unattainable. The higher people place Jesus, the less responsibility humanity owns for failure to reach the level of spiritual development he called everyone to achieve. Playing to the spiritual paralysis of a feckless era, Christian fundamentalists tell the populace to trust Jesus and he'll take care of everything. It is a message that offers some comfort but little real help. Humanity has progressed only by learning to trust its gifts and to work with others for lasting solutions. This is the hard spiritual and intellectual homework required to change lives for the better, and people have often fled from responsibility for their own growth by looking to Jesus as an external savior who alone can make things right.

For 2,000 years people have avoided accountability by awarding the most extraordinary attributes and showering prodigious affection on this simple Jewish teacher from Galilee. Daily, he is the object of an almost boundless adoration. Jesus is loved, emotionally and intellectually, in a manner that nonsubscribers to the Christian religion must find rather peculiar. No other prophet or teacher has evoked this kind of personal rapture on the part of his devotees. The faithful Muslim worships the God of Muhammad not the Prophet himself, which would be a blasphemous idea to Islamic theology. Buddhists are more drawn to the teachings of the compassionate Buddha than to a personal relationship with Gautama Siddhartha. Christians, on the other hand, are a tribe of believers divided by doctrine yet united by devotion to Jesus Christ. As a member of an Eastern religion once remarked to me, not unkindly, "All you Christians agree about *following* Jesus. What you can't seem to agree about is *where he's going*."

This persistent, personal attachment to Jesus is no less than astonishing, considering how distant the man of Nazareth stands from even those who came immediately after him. The distancing process had already begun in the first generation. Jesus spoke incessantly about God; Paul wrote incessantly about Jesus. No one can doubt the primitive church loved Jesus with a passion that required them to keep the faith even if it meant losing their lives. This is even more incredible when we realize that only a tiny handful of people ever heard Jesus speak in the flesh. They did not know the man of Nazareth, but they felt a deep relationship to a spiritual being that they knew as their resurrected Lord. As the lovely old hymn affirms:

"You ask me how I know he lives?
He lives within my heart."[6]

Jesus of Nazareth

The historic Jesus was an ordinary man who led a brief, ordinary life that changed the world. Despite the widespread penchant for identifying the son of Joseph and Mary with the Christ of faith, it is abundantly clear that the supernatural creature whom Christians have adored is not the original Jesus of Nazareth. That man is long gone, another obscure life celebrated in absentia with legend, myth and editorial invention. Beginning in the first generation with Paul of Tarsus, the nimble hands of successive interpreters quickly reshaped the Rabbi Yeshua Ben Josef into *Jesus Christ*, a theological conglomeration of concepts and ideas gathered around the distant, fragmented memories of a historic person. Christian Scriptures offer documents written by second generation followers and provide a glimpse into his life and teachings, but not without heavy editorial input and fill-in-the-blanks fictionalization of the story. The process of Christian myth-building is so readily apparent that the great 20th-century German scholar Rudolf Bultmann called for a counter-process of demythologizing, to return the Gospel to its basic elements by freeing the text of its fictionalized, magicalized content.[7]

As time passed, Jesus of Nazareth became more god than man, the fate of martyred leaders from Caesar to Kennedy, especially figures in religious history. The Jesus of Scripture is a first-century literary character based on the memories of the primitive church, but the Second Testament is no more a true representation of the martyred Rabbi Yeshua than a novel set in ancient Rome about the murder of Caesar would conjure the authentic Gaius Julius.

Although the process of ongoing interpretation is seldom acknowledged, the Jesus available today can best be understood as an interactive figure. Readers interact with many biblical images of the Nazarene, and they approach this procession of Jesuses from the far-flung pathways of the individual histories of each reader. Furthermore, the procession of Jesus-images has been both enriched and tainted by the theologies and politics of each generation. Through this interactive program, people have co-created the best Jesus to suit their needs in every age. No other resource is available. The living Jesus who walked the shores of Galilee has gone to his many mansions, either absorbed by an unfeeling cosmos or ascended above this level to some higher degree of union with God.

People actually study Jesus to learn about the Christ, which some traditions identify with the *Imago Dei* indwelling every sentient being. Nevertheless, it is a solid, empirical fact that humans have made and remade Jesus in their image—physically and emotionally, politically and culturally—and that process has continued unabated since he walked the dusty streets of Roman Judea. The true Nazarene is gone; all that remains are the biblical Jesus and the Christ of Faith, lingering scents of a presence, whispers of love and power, preserved in stories and sayings and myths. To note this historical reality is neither to denigrate Jesus Christ nor decry the ongoing process of reinterpretation; it simply describes all that is possible for followers of Jesus through the ages.

The biblical Jesus exists only in this marketplace/workshop of thought and faith as a dynamic, evolving concept of what it means to be human and divine. On him humanity projects its highest hopes and deepest values, which makes the concept of a universal Christ-indwelling far more important than the historical Jesus of Nazareth ever was. The Christ is a portrait of the highest and best, a canvas on which each generation paints their masterpiece of human potential and divine love. Although Jesus Christ today is a thoroughly fictionalized creation of history, this creative process energizes the ethereal Christ of Faith as he downloads into the contemporary world, like the risen Lord stepping down from a portrait, and when he emerges in contemporary life he comes with power to quicken men and women to follow him in newness of life. The power of the Jesus story transcends its historicity; it is released by devotional prayer, theological speculation, and sociocultural reinterpretation. It is a process to be celebrated rather than lamented.

Way Shower

Jesus Christ has been called, among many things, the Way Shower. As the distillation of the wisdom and spiritual confidence that has been poured into and drawn from the Christ-concept over the centuries, the Jesus Christ of Faith has convinced people that the biblical Jesus knows where everyone is going, because he's been there already. Because all "truth" is interactive, people invariably draw on their resources to find an appropriate model for the day in which they live.

Viewed through this lens, Jesus becomes a renewable resource to discover the best qualities of contemporary humanity. The much-touted, bumper-sticker question, "What would Jesus do?" is really not speculation about the choices a first-century rabbi might endorse but a question about personal behavior in the postmodern age: "What would I do, if I were following my highest values?"

Even with these limitations, the historical figure standing behind the biblical Jesus still steps out of the maze of stained glass windows and hands every generation a set of notes to consider as humans ponder life and faith in their culturally conditioned ways. Sometimes, this primordial Jesus issues a challenge that rings through the ages. For example, his command to grow spiritually—ready or not—is uttered in words that strike the ear like a hammer of futility: "Be perfect, therefore, as your heavenly Father is perfect."[8]

What kind of practical Christianity could be built on that absurd injunction? Yet there it is, undaunted by 2,000 years on the shelves of church libraries. *Perfect?* How does one understand *that* without becoming cynical, frustrated or angry? Is there a parallel verse to modify that one, maybe in Aramaic? How realistic was this Galilean prophet anyway? In fact, could not the whole life of Jesus be summarized as an idealistic fantasy that failed ruinously?

Commonwealth of Holy Typicality

Looking at the historical events on their face value, Jesus represents a life that ended in weakness and humiliation. Paradoxically, one could argue this ignominious defeat constituted his greatest triumph. Nothing could make him abandon kindness and steadfast love, not even an unjust death sentence. He marked the path so well that no matter which fork in life people take, Jesus travels along. "Be perfect" he says, with no hint of hyperbole.

Following so many contradictory demands is a clearly impossible task. Nevertheless, there have always been culturally Christian people who hear his call and attempt to walk the supererogatory path he charted. For his followers, Jesus stills the storms of fear and emptiness, healing minds and hearts with love, and spreading peace that passes all understanding. When the apostle Paul told the church at Corinth, "God was in Christ reconciling the world to Himself,"[9] it probably never occurred to Paul that the only way Jesus could have achieved that lofty goal was by inspiring individuals to a new vision of their potential.

Note that it is God, not Jesus, who is the protagonist in Paul's vision. God comes to Earth as the Christ, who in Paul's mythos is the exalted form of Jesus, the man of Nazareth. Nevertheless, Jesus is one of us in all aspects of humanity. By his life, teachings, death and resurrection-experience, Christ Jesus (Paul's preferred term) demonstrates his divine-human nature and reconciles the world of human consciousness with its destiny in the common-wealth of holy typicality, where God-consciousness engulfs men and women as if they were fish in the divine ocean.

With its broad vision of cultural and historical evolution, post-modern Christianity now has the opportunity to see the Lordship of Jesus Christ flowing from the same Source that nourished Buddha, Lao Tzu, Moses, Confucius, Mahavira, Muhammad, Bahá'u'lláh and countless lesser-known men and women. Christians call this fountainhead of divine power and love the Christ, which can also be identified as *Imago Dei*, the divine life-force indwelling all sentient beings. One might reasonably con-tend that all creatures in the cosmos live, move and have their being through this animating God-within. More importantly, through this indwelling divinity humans know the power of love. Women and men are love-capable beings because they are chil-dren of God, made in the *Imago Dei*, which is love itself.

Teddy Bears and Starships

Even for a relatively new species, human beings seem to have elected love as their major study in the divine University of the Cosmos. People love to love and be loved. Human love seems capable of projecting its warmth on all sorts of objects. People love teddy bears and national emblems and sweet melodies. A baby's smile stirs us deeply; even the child of strangers touches the love chords in the mind-heart organ. Men and women are able to love irrationally, deeply, sometimes with a degree of stead-fastness to surpass the loyalty of angels. It is not surprising that humanity would turn its love-light onto the collective personifications of human goodness—the gods and goddesses, divine power, however understood. The religious literature of humanity teems with declarations of devotion, loyalty and affection for the Divine. People need a divine teddy bear, an image to love and cling to and trust when the cosmos goes mad, as it always does from time to time.

Jesus was a man, so he makes an even more convenient target for the Cupid arrows of spiritual adoration, a manageable package of divinity, colored and shaped by the changing tides of world consciousness. Nuns call him *husband;* millions call him *Lord.* The biblical Jesus blesses everyone's inner child; the believer eagerly climbs into his lap and feels secure in the divine embrace. Martyrs in the Roman arena loved him, as did medieval peasants, Renaissance artisans, free-thinkers of the Enlightenment, 19th-century superliterates and revolutionaries, veterans of the world wars and moon-landing astronauts.

Someday, when starships sail the corridors of space at faster-than-light velocities, they will leave earth orbit with Bibles in their prayer chapels. Doubtless there will be churches on the moon and Mars and unknown worlds beyond Orion's belt, along with an assortment of temples, mosques and synagogues too. Humans are irrevocably religious. It is not impossible that someday the great-great-great-whatever-grandchild of someone reading this book will join an alien religion as soon as humans begin encountering them, and perhaps—turning Paul's sermon on Mars Hill in a direction the apostle never envisioned—become the first human-born priest or priestess of a truly Unknown God.

Jesus 2.1–Interactive, Postmodern Paradigm

The only seeing we have is seeing from a perspective; the only knowledge we have is knowledge from a perspective.[1]

—Friedrich Nietzsche

The premise under consideration in this book is that Jesus, as experienced today, is an interactive work in progress, co-created by people from the data provided by Scripture, tradition and life experiences, and processed by their powers of intellectual reasoning and creative intuition. It is a solid, historical fact that humans have made and remade the Nazarene in their image—physically and emotionally, politically and culturally—throughout the centuries since he walked the dusty streets of Roman Judea.

Although Jesus Christ has been a thoroughly interactive figure throughout history, the postmodern age has finally produced a paradigm to explain this phenomenon: the computer program upgrade. Arriving after the initial software has been installed, an upgrade builds on the platform already laid down and modifies the program to improve basic functions or add new features that were unimaginable when the first edition hit the market. Later upgrades will continue the process. This is, of course, exactly what has happened to the earlier "program" built on the life and teachings of Jesus Christ. Every generation has tweaked the Jesus model until it harmonized with the issues and requirements specific to the times.

At first glance, some might call this a cynical attitude. One could reasonably argue that the goal should not be to remake Jesus in anyone's image but to discover his authentic message and conform yourself accordingly. Of course, every church believes this is exactly what it has done, but the crazy-quilt landscape of Christendom shows otherwise. While people are understandably devoted to the search for a historical Jesus, many of whom are respected biblical scholars and theologians, nevertheless the inescapable conclusion from a study of Jesus as an interactive figure will show that embedded theological assumptions, which scholars inevitably bring to the Bible, will *always* shape the results of their quest. Even if one were to allow that the Jesus Seminar has actually discovered some of the "authentic" sayings of Jesus through scholarly review of the Gospel texts, all the mechanics of postmodern socialization come into play as soon as the question moves from "What did he say?" to "What does that mean for us today?"

Subtitling this study *An Upgrade for the 21st Century* underscores the theological process that continues unabated in the new millennium. An interactive Jesus is not only unavoidable; the model also has great advantages. It allows humanity to project the highest and best attributes of its character on a recognizable figure and follow the leader in the direction that most people already know they should be traveling. Although Jesus has been portrayed as a lofty king with groveling subjects—a divine emperor who has no problem with subjugated servants or even slavery itself—today it is possible to say that Jesus loves humanity because he is humanity, the best example of what it means to be human and divine. In the 21st century humans have learned, by and large, that subjugation and slavery are not acts blessed by godly sanction.

Light, Not the Lamp

Understanding Jesus as interactive allows creative flexibility, and the outcome is never certain. Although hindsight clearly marks a chosen highway as the obvious choice, looking ahead where the road divides presents a traveler with live options. Often, as in Robert Frost's great poem "The Road Not Taken," both paths have advantages and disadvantages, a circumstance that behavioral scientists call a *double approach-avoidance conflict*.

In making initial adjustments to the recorded memories of a living, historical Jesus, the developing Christian church faced such a double approach-avoidance conflict, because both positive (approach) and negative (avoidance) results followed once some-one decided to cast Jesus either as human or divine. The proto-orthodox party—those who would one day hold the majority opinion—avoided the dual temptations, declaring Jesus neither exclusively divine nor exclusively human. Too limiting, they insisted, because Jesus was both human and divine. Traditional theology still insists that Jesus Christ must be fully human for his divinity to be accessible to mere mortals. However, this proposi-tion—the uniqueness of Jesus' divine-human nature—is arguably not a mandatory component of Christology.

There are other alternatives that are far kinder to humanity and historically far more tenable. Postmodern men and women have generally given up on God as the old man in the sky of Renaissance art. They know there is no cosmic Christ who, according to memorized creed, "sitteth at the right hand of God the Father." Mystics through the ages have found something bet-ter, an inner Christ enthroned in every man and woman, and from this inner repository men and women have discovered that God brings forth anew the perfect idea of what it means to be human and divine in all times and seasons of life. It is this inner, divine spark that poets and prophets have recognized throughout history, although the tendency has persisted to confuse the lamp with the light.

Danger Zone: Discussing Religion

When addressing epistemology or cosmology, in fact, when looking at all the grand questions of life, the starting point for postmodern Christian thought can be clarified by this vital distinction between the external lamp of Jesus and the inner light, which is the Christ-presence in every sentient being. While *Jesus 2.1* definitely allows people to modify their understanding of Jesus, some would rightly argue for an interactive model that requires communication in both directions. Modern interpreters have an obligation to hear what the authors of the Second Testament were actually saying about the primordial Jesus of Scripture. This process of clarification brings up an important point, namely, the distinction between *descriptive* and *prescriptive* theology. We have been doing both in this study so far, describing what exists and prescribing possible choices or alternative points of view.

Fairly early in life, most people learn that it can be dangerous to discuss religion with friends and family. Many people have set beliefs and will suffer no challenges to the world as they see it. Yet life is growth, and growth means change, which is one of the reasons Bishop John Shelby Spong has written that Christianity must either change or die. Effective religion is always a work in progress, responding to the times and circumstances of real people in a real world. In this need for flexibility and responsiveness, religion is not unlike the other taboo subject that popular wisdom warns us against discussing—politics.

Ballot-Boxed in Georgia

True confession: In a previous incarnation—well, at least a few years ago—I ran in a partisan political election. I was the 1992 Democratic nominee for the majority Republican 114th District of the Georgia House of Representatives. Local Democrats were graciously willing to let a carpetbagger Yankee like me fall in battle against an incumbent who would have otherwise retained his seat in an uncontested election. I think the contest at least provided some comic relief for my fellow Georgians. Fortunately for the Peach State, the voters of my district chose the other guy—but I learned so much! The process of representative government really comes alive once citizens take the time to get involved in the elections. I eventually became an appointed member of the Richmond County Board of Elections and was able to serve all the people as an overseer of the elective process.

During my brief sojourn into partisan politics I learned that, contrary to popular belief, the political arena is not dominated by knaves and scoundrels but by men and women with sincerely held, albeit conflicting, social, cultural and economic values. Good politicians learn how to function in the real world by compromise, reinterpretation and coalition. In a utopian world, whenever a problem presented itself, everyone would agree and their voices rise in a harmonious finale. Human history suggests people won't be living in utopia until later in the program. Even in the best possible scenarios, progressively self-perfecting people will struggle to achieve worthwhile goals while limiting each other's excesses through checks and balances.

Vote for Jesus?

The same human dynamics were in play when Christianity was born. Hellenistic paganism and the new Christian faith quickly merged because they were never apart; they sprang from the same milieu. Although a cursory glance at church history might suggest the Christianizing process flowed from a Jewish Jesus who exerted a powerful influence on the pagan world, in reality the communication was multifaceted. When Christianity reached out from its Jewish homeland, the mingling of various schools of Jewish Christian thought with Hellenistic ideas was unavoidable, even desirable, as the two worlds cross-pollinated. Greek-speaking people around the Mediterranean basin, who were accustomed to listening to the campaign rhetoric from mystery cults and assorted sects representing this or that god or goddess, found themselves drawn to the issues and answers proposed by Paul and other Christian missionaries. They decided in large numbers to cast their lot with the man of Nazareth, but it was a free choice in a milieu that understood the value of pluralism.

This is one of the points that Jihadists and all other fundamentalists of today fail to recognize, i.e., the interactive nature of world cultures. As the human population becomes more aware of this cultural dynamic, the evolutionary penalty for religious worldviews that try to fight the movement toward higher consciousness might very well be extinction. Although theology is no longer called "the queen of the sciences," theologians attempting to discuss a subject as deep and far-ranging as Christology can only command respect for the quality of their work by establishing ground rules and clarifying the methodology they will follow.

So let's take a moment to do some methodological groundwork now. Authentic theology contains two basic elements, descriptive and prescriptive.

Descriptive Vs. Prescriptive Theology

A *descriptive* analysis tries to explain what a particular belief or practice means. This is best illustrated by biblical theology, where the task of scholarship is to determine what the author of a particular passage was probably saying to his ancient target audience. A descriptive analysis of the sacrament of baptism might also attempt to clarify the practices of initiation into the Christian community and the beliefs which this or that group has held about baptism. Depending on the theological background of the group being addressed, even basic terms may have to be described. In some traditions, calling baptism a sacrament (rather than an ordinance) requires an explanation, and if the goal is to illustrate rather than advocate, the process is descriptive.

Prescriptive reasoning attempts to push beyond clarification about the way things are and to articulate underlying causes, discover connections and arrive at new possibilities. In its most radical form, prescriptive theology says, "You have heard that it was said, 'You shall love your neighbor and hate your enemy.' But I say to you, Love your enemies and pray for those who persecute you" (Mt. 5:43-44).

Descriptive and prescriptive theology can be objective or subjective, although describing what exists is ostensibly more impartial than prescribing new connections. Frequently these two methodologies are mixed haphazardly by artless commentators, so the reader bumps along over description and prescription without realizing the road has been cobbled together with incompatible materials. The reason for this amalgamation is clear. For theologians, both amateur and professional, it is exquisitely tempting to favor one's point of view by discovering it embedded in the words of Jesus, Saint Paul, Thomas Aquinas or Gandhi. The more deeply people hold a certain conviction, the more easily they can "discover" authoritative support for that idea elsewhere.

An honest respect for methodology requires a beginning point within a self-consciously objective, descriptive model of the sources—facilitated by studying the Bible, noncanonical scriptures, and other historical documents of the faith; reflecting on

the beliefs and practices of Christian and other religious communities throughout the ages; and surveying other resources now
available due to the explosion of knowledge in this computer-
enhanced world society—then to advance prescriptively by offering new insights for students of theology today. Although this
does not require a rigid formula—first descriptive, then prescriptive—it obliges religious thinkers to be aware of the perils of
unsubstantiated speculation and to acknowledge when the line
between *explaining* and *advocating* has been crossed, as it will be
in almost any theological work, the present volume included.

Jesus 2.1 continues the pattern established in my volume on
systematic theology, *Glimpses of Truth*. While attempting some
degree of objectivity, especially when doing descriptive theology,
this work proceeds from a point of view within the
progressive/liberal circle of Christian faith. Drawing on the
insights from a wide range of traditions, I would nevertheless be
remiss if I did not begin by declaring my home base resides in
Metaphysical Christianity, as viewed through a postmodern,
panentheistic, process theology lens. That said, I will still attempt
to apply some degree of intellectual rigor to the study of
Christology and place the insights of Metaphysical Christianity in
touch and in context with mainstream theologies of the early 21st
century.

With these first thoughts and observations in mind, let's continue investigating Christology by taking an imaginative look at
the guy under the halo, which I have entitled "Dream a Little
Dream With Me."

Dream a Little
Dream With Me ...

I do not know of a single reputable New
Testament scholar in the world who thinks that
the stories of Jesus' virginal birth are actually historical or that the resuscitation of a deceased
physical body is the meaning of resurrection.[1]

—Bishop John Shelby Spong

Imagine what might happen if Jesus Christ walked the streets
today like an ordinary guy. No fanfare, neither golden trumpets
nor heavenly choruses. Jesus just strolls into First Downtown
Church, right off Main Street, on a little inspection tour. Does the
humble Jewish carpenter recognize himself in the superhuman
figure that humans have created in his name? Is Jesus pleased
with what people have done with the message he entrusted to
them 2,000 years ago? Does he smile at what his followers have
built—in his name—and say, "Well done, thou good and faithful
servants"?

Not even close.

More likely, he is amazed and probably appalled that
Christians capitalize the personal pronoun when referring to him.
The newly arrived Jesus gazes, dumbfounded, at the bizarre
assortment of cultic, cultural and ceremonial institutions operated by people who claim to be his followers. As an advocate of
the poor, he is scandalized at jeweled basilicas that have risen to
honor him while homeless children sleep outside cathedral doors.

Jesus glares at the warring *Christ*-ian sects, each claiming to have exclusive access to him, and is profoundly disturbed by their mixture of condescension and condemnation when confronting non-Christians. Most of all, as a good Jew, he finds the prayers to him as the unique Son of God—elevating him to membership in a triune Godhead, making him the equivalent to God Almighty—to be nothing less than blasphemous. When church members invoke his name in prayer as if he were a deity, Yeshua Ben Josef can endure no more. He shouts, "Abomination!" and tears his garments and flees the building.

What has happened to the mortal who walked among his kind? How did this unpretentious Nazarene become more than divine, to the point where Karl Barth was able to say that when people think "God" they need to think "Jesus Christ" again and again? How did one solitary life take on such metaphysical significance that serious-minded men and women spent generations arguing about how completely his being was subsumed in the Divine: two Natures, one Will? What instigated the eternal bantering about the way he was begotten, the meaning of his death and the "work" of Jesus upon the cross? People who knew Jesus in the flesh would not recognize him in those religio-technical debates.

Imagine a new archaeological discovery, a newly opened Palestinian tomb containing sealed jars with manuscripts written by contemporaries of Jesus. If you are willing to tap into the imaginative quality that dramatists call the willing suspension of disbelief, permit me the following fictionalized speculations. First, here's something a boyhood friend might say after hearing a disciple proclaim that the resurrected Christ Jesus was one with the Father:

Are you possessed of a demon? You're a Jew, yet you say Yeshua was the God of Israel, walking the earth? I knew him. He was one of us, the son of Joseph and Mary. He worked in that shop— see? Right across the street. I remember, when he was little, his father spanked him for dropping a new batch of bricks one-by-one off the miller's roof. His favorite game was a rowdy wrestling match with other boys of Nazareth. And sometimes he got mad and bit you if he was losing.

Another friend recalled:

When he grew into a young man, all his neighbors knew how he hungered for Miriam, the daughter of the village butcher. I saw him secretly watching her from his shop as she passed. Miriam was more obvious, rather openly admiring his muscled torso whenever the young house builder worked in her vicinity. Yeshua was too shy—he never spoke to her, but he told me he dreamed about holding her in the night. Poor boy, so smitten he couldn't concentrate. Working in the carpenter shop that year, he accidentally smashed his thumb several times.

His cousin remembered with a smile:

Whenever Yeshua slammed his fingers with a hammer, he blurted a string of curses that would have gotten him stoned to death in the days of Moses. He was an ordinary man, who slept and ate. He liked wine and grilled lamb with leeks. And he relieved himself of bodily wastes like

every other man of Nazareth. I liked him. I
mourn his death. But God among us? Hardly.

One of the village elders at Nazareth might have said:

Well, the whole idea is ridiculous! In what possible way was this sun-darkened, tough-limbed
laborer, God walking among us? He didn't even
know Hebrew well enough to be a teacher at our
Synagogue! And we knew all about his mother.
Shameful! Only a kindly old man like Joseph
would have raised the boy, considering ... well,
you know.

Finally, listen to a Roman centurion:

Now they're saying this Jesus was divine. Can
you imagine offering wine and incense to his
shabby image? Making him a god is an insult to
Mount Olympus. What kind of pantheon would
admit an executed Jewish bastard? If Yeshua Ben
Josef is God, everybody is!

Imago Dei

Of course, that's exactly the point where this historical-critical
study of the God-man begins to make sense to the postmodern
mind, with the frank assertion that Jesus of Nazareth was not a
demigod or special incarnation from on high, but a human being
in whom some people have detected the signature of divinity, the
Imago Dei. Whereas some historic Christologies have argued that
Jesus must be uniquely God in order to save fallen humanity, others have argued that if Jesus were anything more than typically
human it would render him so transcendent as to be useless to
ordinary mortals. It is reasonable to expect a Supreme Being to be
All-Forgiving, All-Loving, All-Nice. *Forgive your enemies?* Not a

problem for the Lord of Hosts. *Love God with all your heart, mind and strength?* God should have a good attitude about himself, don't you think? If Jesus is the unique Son of God, co-equal with the Father, begotten from the beginning of time, Second Person of the Trinity, through whom all things were made—how could anyone hope to follow him?

If Jesus is uniquely God—Jesus and Jesus alone—then he is, for all practical purposes, utterly useless to human beings in their struggle for self-betterment. In fact, Jesus as God Almighty is less than useless; he is an insult, an affront to human imperfection, a flaunting of Divine Goodness in the face of humanity's wars and rumors of wars. If Jesus is God in a unique and unattainable way, he is like a billboard touting the good life to people trapped in the slums, a divine mirage that beckons but never rewards, taunting humanity, whose mortal lips are unworthy, with a drink of living waters.

This was Luther's well-documented dilemma. Before he discovered the Pauline doctrine of justification by faith, the future father of Protestantism was a guilt-ridden Augustinian monk. He found that nothing he could do would free him from the tendency to err again. And, Luther reasoned, since God hated *sin*, God must hate *him*. Driven to excess of penitence and confession, obsessed with his sinfulness in the face of Divine Perfection, Martin Luther told his confessor that he was ready to retaliate: Luther now hated God. It was in the depths of this self-hatred and rejection of God's mercy that he had his "tower experience" breakthrough.

Luther often poured over the Scriptures alone, late and at length. The story goes that one night he was "studying in his office, which was on the third floor of a tower built into the city wall of Wittenberg"[2] when he came upon a passage in the first chapter of Paul's Letter to the Romans, which itself quoted a text from the rather obscure book of Habakkuk in the Hebrew Bible.

The prophet Habakkuk, like Luther, had climbed a tower to survey the landscape of his mind, but the prophet had come down from his ramparts with a powerful message: "The righteous live by their faith."[3]

Luther suddenly realized God did not require him to reach perfection through his efforts at holiness, but to raise his consciousness and accept his acceptance. It is also possible to interpret "justification by faith" by the language Paul used a few chapters later: "Do not be conformed to this world, but be transformed by the renewing of your minds."[4] Perfect conduct is not required for Divine approval, because God does not disapprove of humans in the first place.

Luther remained a child of his culture and was still suffering from highly adverse personal experiences; he never completely shook free of his stick-beating parents. His God remained a punishing, wrathful deity whose anger blazed at all those who did not accept the Truth—which, coincidentally, was identical with Luther's theology. He was certain the blood of Jesus Christ had cleansed him from sin as a free gift from God in exchange for faith in this atoning act. Without such a sacrifice by Jesus, Luther believed that every soul would be doomed to fiery, eternal hell. He believed the atonement was accessed by "faith" (intellectual assent).

Postmodern Christians might find grave inconsistencies in this turn-or-burn theology. How is someone "washed clean by His blood" any closer to godliness than before conversion? According to Luther and his ancient antecedent, Saint Augustine, the convert is from a broken, miserable, incomplete creature before conversion. Accepting Jesus Christ as Lord and Savior opens the door to heaven, but what if the person lingers in sin until experiencing a deathbed conversion? Does that mean a broken, miserable and incomplete creature is set loose in paradise? Changing the rules to admit sinful people, who are not spiritually qualified, into a supposedly "perfect" heavenly city would be like pardoning all the murderers on death row and turning them loose in the streets because they promised not to do it again. Unless the person has experienced real growth and learned how to overcome the destructive, self-defeating tendencies that landed him on death row, none but a society of lunatics would throw open the prison doors based on the convicted killers' pledge to behave themselves. It begins to sound like cheap grace, as Dietrich Bonhoeffer called it.[5] Salvation by faith alone doesn't bridge the gap between Luther's view of unassailable Divine heights and incorrigible, inescapable human inadequacy. A cleaned-up sinner is a sinner still.

Of course, Augustine's answer was that people cannot even choose their own salvation; God changes and transforms people based on his righteous Will. Augustine's response opened a Pandora's Box of questions involving freedom, predestination, and the Creator-creature relationship, all of which have been discussed and debated *ad nauseam*. Rather than gallop into that minefield, an alternative route should probably be sought.

At the risk of sounding presumptuous, one might legitimately ask if God's love for humanity does not imply some degree of divine responsibility for human spiritual development. Simply "saving" humanity is not enough. What sort of parent rescues his children from their mistakes without requiring them to learn the lessons necessary to avoid the next catastrophe? Conservative churches have a point when they insist that sin has its consequences, and that even a merciful God cannot unilaterally fix bad choices without making a mockery of Divine justice and free will.

The notion that God punishes anyone for anything is a vestige of the ancient worldview, where the court of the oriental despot was the model for God on His judgment throne in heaven. The boy Luther cowers in the dark corner of his room, waiting for his caning after stealing a walnut from the pantry. God punishes those who don't behave or don't get their theological thinking right, and the beatings he summons for the damned at the hands of his demon surrogates are far worse, infinitely crueler, than any child abuse dispensed by medieval human parents.

Another point worth considering is whether all this language about God-out-there makes any sense whatsoever. If God is found not in some distant heaven but in the depths of existence, if God is the very energy that empowers thought and life and love, perhaps what Luther discovered was not so much a path to Jehovah on the throne as it was a way for the divine-within to accept itself as worthy of love.

Dust or Spirit?

The Jesus Christ model provides a starting point to access the discussion about the value and purpose of life. When asking "What is God like?" people are really asking, "What is the nature of Reality?" Is there meaning and purpose in life, or is consciousness a mere fluke, a moment spent streaking through the light, bracketed by eternal darkness? And if life has purpose, what is it? Obedience, achievement, enjoyment, self-sacrifice, creativity, suffering, purity, ecstasy or service?

The solution to the problem of balancing God's mercy and justice must be found in a world where, at least in the short run, the good guys don't always win. Faith operates in moments of apparent disaster and futility. Jesus of Nazareth showed exactly that kind of faith, even to forgiving his tormentors in the last hours of his life. If this man were God's solitary incarnation on Earth, a unique expression of divinity, the gesture is benevolent but empty of ethical content.

If sentient beings are both human and divine, and if Jesus demonstrated this indwelling divinity to show humankind the way it must travel eventually, then the reconciling acts of his life, death and resurrection experience become a signpost for humanity. If he did it, everyone can go and do likewise.

There is a crucial question Christianity must face if it is to survive in a pluralistic, postmodern, space-faring, multispecies cosmos: Are humans creatures of the dust, bond-servants of a jealous God, or are they creative expressions of Spirit, sisters and brothers in divine consciousness with all sentient beings, blossoming from the same energy that formed all matter and empowers everything to be?

On Being a Christian

To be more precise, the above is not so much an objectively stated question as a statement disguised in an interrogative form. Let me rephrase the presenting problem as a real question: In practical terms, what is special about being a "Christian" in the 21st century? After all, life introduces its mysteries to everyone. Like Jesus of Nazareth, all humans are physical/spiritual beings who are born, live and die. Like Jesus, every person sooner or later ponders the meaning and purpose of life. Humans often speculate on the nature of human consciousness and its destiny after death. Some have looked deeper, searching for ways to overcome the design flaws in the species that have produced such glaring contradictions as love and hate, peace and war, friendship and bigotry, altruism and hoarding. Many of the models that have served humanity have been found through an examination of Jesus of Nazareth.

An elder brother has been through this long before each generation was born, and he has much to say about the human condition and destiny. By definition, "Christian" theology holds that the life and teachings of Jesus the Christ must somehow provide answers to these profound dilemmas. In his benchmark book, *On*

Being a Christian, Catholic theologian Hans Küng goes as far as to declare that a Christian is anyone for whom Jesus is somehow definitive of God and humanity; anyone who looks to Jesus Christ to discern the nature of God and the potential within each human, is by definition a *Christ*-ian:

> A Christian is not just any human being with genuine conviction, sincere faith and good will. No one can fail to see that genuine conviction, sincere faith and good will exist also outside Christianity. But all those can be called Christians for whom in life and death Jesus Christ is ultimately decisive.[6]

It is easy to hear the voice of intellectual courage in Küng. It is also easy to understand how the good professor landed in hot water with official Vatican doctrine, which might be why some progressive Christians admire him. Some traditionalists, however, see Küng as a threat to the faith. Permit me a personal example to illustrate.

Twenty years ago, my wife, Carol-Jean, and I were riding a train across the wooded German countryside. We shared one of those classic European compartments with a thin young man in black, with whom I soon found myself engaged in a pleasant conversation. He spoke no English, and I am not fluent in German, but luckily he was patient enough to repeat and paraphrase until I understood him. I discovered that he worked as a repair technician on pipe organs for some of the great houses of worship on the continent. It was fascinating to hear how the huge pipe organs were kept running, and our conversation was cordial at first. Then, since I was reading *On Being A Christian* at the time and knew Dr. Küng was teaching at Tübingen University, I asked the young musical technician if he'd ever met the great Catholic professor.

His demeanor changed, and he literally snarled, *"Küng? Küng ist ein häretiker!"*

Even my wife, Carol-Jean, whose German vocabulary could be charitably described as not terribly robust, totally got what the young Catholic was saying. This lad, who spent his life traveling from cathedral to cathedral maintaining the great pipe organs of Europe, was a devout, traditionalist Catholic. To him, the free-thinking Küng was no scholar of the Church but a faithless, subversive heretic. I changed the subject, and we continued our pleasant chat. The encounter reminded me that religious fervor is not the sole province of Islamic fundamentalists or preachers at fire-and-brimstone tent meetings.

Everyone has a system of beliefs. The atheist who declares disbelief in God is operating from a faith-based system as surely as the Greek Orthodox monk meditating below the crucifix in his monastery cell on an Aegean island; or the Shinto priest burning incense and ministering to his shrines at Kyoto; or the Muslim walking a circle around the *Kiblah* to fulfill the obligation of Pilgrimage to Mecca and become a *Hajji*; or the Hindu mother dipping her child in the Holy Ganges and offering fruit and prayer to a medley of gods and goddesses, all of whom she knows are aspects of the One Presence and One Power. Belief in no god is belief nonetheless.

The Metaphysics of Atheism

Ralph Waldo Emerson said people have no choice but to be religious: "A man will worship something—have no doubt about that."[7] This sweeping generalization includes the whole spectrum of humanity, from people who regularly ponder and meditate on the Divine to those who never contemplate religious subjects. Everyone has a worldview that incorporates "religious" beliefs about life, death and the nature of reality, which is another way of saying that everyone has a metaphysical system.

The irony is that even rejecting faith requires faith. Atheism is itself a belief system with metaphysical presumptions that function like the tenets of any other religion. Atheists place their faith in the belief that God is *not* real; Jews, Christians and Muslims place their faith in the belief that God *is* real. Neither believers nor atheists can prove the point. Both operate from unspoken assumptions about life, death, humanity and the cosmos, none of which can be verified with scientific dependability. In fact, most atheists pay unintentional homage to the traditional Christian God, since he is ordinarily the Supreme Being whom they reject.

The atheists I have known have rarely proclaimed their disbelief in the pantheon of lesser celestial personalities from Catholic and Protestant lore—the Angel Gabriel, the Virgin Mary or Saint Francis of Assisi. Nonbelievers seldom bother to dismiss divine beings from Asian religions (like *Buddha, Siva* and *Kali)*, or the Olympian deities (including *Zeus, Apollo* and *Athena)*, or the Norse gods (*Odin, Loki, Thor*, et al). Now, to return to the computer metaphor, it is specifically the *YHWH* of Sinai program they rejoice in uninstalling, although some have a denunciation patch available for Jesus and offer an optional anti-Allah upgrade for post-9/11 atheists.

What this suggests is that all worldviews, even atheism, are grounded in a system of life experiences, secondhand information and faith in things unseen. Operating from a broader view of what constitutes *religion*, one could argue, with Emerson, that every worldview is inherently religious. Emerson writes:

> The gods we worship write their names on our
> faces, be sure of that. ... [A man] may think that
> his tribute is paid in secret in the dark recesses of
> his heart—but it will out. That which dominates

will determine his life and character. Therefore, it behooves us to be careful what we worship, for what we are worshipping we are becoming.[8]

I hold the appropriate theological response to the above is "Wow!" Emerson astutely observed that whenever a person cherishes something above all else, values it ultimately, that particular *something* has become an object of worship, in effect, a god. The gods of everyday life may not part the Red Sea or ride the clouds of heaven, but they provide a framework of meaning and value without which a person would feel lost.

Everyone must have some sort of belief system, even an atheistic one, because life requires people to function in a complex world in which they cannot know everything. Today's men and women believe all sorts of things about which they can have little personal knowledge. Most Europeans believe there is a Great Wall of China, even if they've never seen that vast barrier with their naked eyes. Most people today believe in justice, equality and some form of the Golden Rule, even though these ideas are abstract concepts that cannot be examined under a microscope. Sometimes, people believe all sorts of things, without regard to demonstrable reality, as in the hackneyed joke about places in the American hinterlands where folks believe the moon landings were faked and professional wrestling is real. In all these cases the same dynamic applies: life in a complex information age requires people to take on faith what cannot possibly be known from personal experience. Everyone's mind is steeped in belief.

Ground of Our Being

Theologian Paul Tillich provided an excellent model for understanding the human religious mind when he contended that religion was found in those places which concern us ultimately. Anything that is ultimately important to us will paint a portrait of God and of religious faith. For Tillich, God is not some Being "out there" beyond the skies, a supernatural First Citizen of the cosmos; God is the "Ground of our being," the very power of existence itself. Tillich writes:

> The name of this infinite and inexhaustible depth and ground of all Being is God. That depth is what the word God means. And if that word has not much meaning for you, translate it, and speak of the depths of your life, of the source of your being, of your ultimate concerns, of what you take seriously without any reservation.[9]

What does such a radical view of God mean to men and women living in the 21st century? For openers, it means they may have to shuck all that God's-in-his-Heaven-all's-right-with-the-world language. Tillich was a German theologian who escaped Hitler's wrath by fleeing to teach in North America before World War II began in earnest. He had seen his world turn topsy-turvy: The German nation—arguably the most highly educated, cultured people on the European continent—turned over its reins of power to a howling mass of Nazis who would lead them to ruin and commit atrocities unprecedented even in a world plagued by endless warfare. Tillich openly opposed the Nazis, so it was not surprising that in his theological writing he was unafraid to challenge the highest power of them all: Not just Hitler, but God on His throne. If unchecked power was unacceptable, then the greatest arbitrary authority of them all, the King of Heaven, had to go. By sacrificing these radically different yet equally false gods—demonic Hitler and good God Jehovah—Tillich made room for another God-concept when he challenged believers and atheists to deny that life has any depth, purpose or meaning:

> ... you must forget everything traditional that you have learned about God, perhaps even that

> word itself. For if you know that God means
> depth, you know much about him. You cannot
> then call yourself an atheist or unbeliever. For
> you cannot think or say: Life has no depth! Life is
> shallow. Being itself is surface only. If you could
> say this with complete seriousness, you would
> be an atheist; but otherwise you are not. He who
> knows about depth knows about God.[10]

What is ultimately important to humans in the 21st century? Easy answers come to mind, but they are quickly dismissed as less than ultimate. Friends and family, vital as they are to human well-being, can be taken from us and life will go painfully on. The same is true with health, wealth and even happiness. These are important aspects of life, but not Ultimate Concerns. When raising the bar to the level of Ultimate Concerns, there can be only one answer: Humanity's relationship to God and the resulting spiritual growth experienced from this communion with the One Presence/One Power is the lone element in consciousness that cannot adequately be replaced by anything. This is a possible meaning of the enigmatic words purportedly spoken by Jesus to his disciples:

> He who loves father or mother more than me is
> not worthy of me; and he who loves son or
> daughter more than me is not worthy of me; and
> he who does not take up his cross and follow me
> is not worthy of me. He who finds his life will
> lose it, and he who loses his life for my sake will
> find it.[11]

In this passage Jesus is most likely not calling people to abandon their loved ones; he is pointing out the difference between that which concerns us ultimately and every other kind of relationship. By announcing that any person who "finds his life will lose it," the text seems to suggest the shallowness of trying to make anything Ultimate but God, Who must ultimately be the center of life.

Yet, in raising this issue, the biblical Jesus has challenged humanity to consider the relationship people should have with himself. If God is found in the depths of human existence, not the heights of clouds in heaven, and if God is that which concerns us ultimately, the intellectually honest person must ask what part Jesus Christ plays in this grand view of the Divine. Why relegate such significant relationships—father, mother, son and daughter—to secondary status and first seek God through companionship with him? In what way is something of the unseen Divine revealed in the life, death, resurrection-experience, teaching and proclamation of Jesus Christ? According to Matthew's Gospel, it is not a new question:

> He came to his hometown and began to teach the people in their synagogue, so that they were astounded and said, "Where did this man get this wisdom and these deeds of power? Is not this the carpenter's son? Is not his mother called Mary? And are not his brothers James and Joseph and Simon and Judas? And are not all his sisters with us? Where then did this man get all this?" And they took offense at him.[12]

A brief look at the nature of metaphysical studies and the process of theological reflection are appropriate before plunging into an extensive study of Christology as an interactive enterprise.

Practical Christianity, Metaphysics and Theology

Central Metaphysical Principle: OP²

Metaphysical is a generally misunderstood and frequently abused adjective these days. It has been conjured up when discussing everything from the Eucharist to witchcraft. Its noun form, *metaphysics,* originated in a misreading of Aristotle, whose writings on the measurable cosmos (physics) preceded his speculations of the underlying nature of existence itself. Since this section followed physics, it was listed in the historically significant Andronikas Edition (70 BCE) under the heading *meta-physics* (Greek, *meta,* meaning "beyond" or "after"). The use of the term is entirely accidental; Aristotle never employed it. He did, however, develop a grand view of Reality, to which later interpreters would apply the misnomer "Aristotle's Metaphysic."

When philosophers and theologians use the word, it is generally in this technical sense, i.e., metaphysics is "an attempt to characterize existence or reality as a whole, instead of, as in the various natural sciences, particular parts or aspects thereof."[1] Metaphysics can also mean "an attempt to explore the realm of the suprasensible, beyond the world of experience; to establish indubitable first principles as a foundation for all other knowledge; or to critically examine what more limited studies simply take for granted."[2] This secondary definition stands closer to the way Charles Fillmore described the subject:

> Metaphysics—The systematic study of the science of Being; that which transcends the

physical. By pure metaphysics is meant a clear understanding of the realm of ideas and their legitimate expression.[3]

Notice how Fillmore's definition tries to invoke the pseudo-Aristotelian sense of the word: metaphysics involves study of "that which transcends the physical." Not content with cutting the mental undergrowth from the whole jungle of possible meanings, Fillmore wants a field with well-defined boundaries for his metaphysical Christianity. He narrows the definition by specifying that "pure metaphysics" involves reaching a "clear understanding" of the nature of ultimate reality as "the realm of ideas," which when properly applied will outpicture as the "legitimate expression" of the workings of those Divine Principles. In other words, a metaphysical Christianity will help people live more effective lives in the here-and-now because it operates from certain principles that can demonstrate their truth by personal application. It must first and foremost be a practical Christianity. As the Twelve Step recovery literature says, "It works if you work it."[4]

The central principle that underlies such a practical Christian belief system is often expressed in the phrase: "There is only one Presence and one Power in the universe, God, the Good omnipotent."[5] One Presence/One Power, which in my work is often designated by the symbol OP^2, is so definitive for Practical Christianity that it literally draws the circle of faith within which this theology functions. I find the concept so elemental that I've made a sign for my wall:

ONE PRINCIPLE: ONE PRESENCE, ONE POWER

EVERYTHING ELSE IS COMMENTARY.

OP^2 as a foundation principle has implications for Christology that are quite liberating, as will presently become apparent. Before launching into the vast sea of theological exploration, the first task is to clarify what the word *theology* means.

Theology and Other Religious Studies

Glimpses of Truth offered the following working definition:

> THEOLOGY: Organized, rational reflection on ideas and practices pertaining to the Divine, God and Ultimate Concerns, evaluated from within the boundaries of a chosen circle of faith.[6]

When participants in a religious tradition reflect upon any aspect of their beliefs and religious practices in an organized, rational manner, they are doing *theology*. Since by definition theological reflection begins within a community of shared ideas and practices, a circle of faith, theology differs from other forms of enquiry into spiritual thought and behavior, such as cultural anthropology, sociology, social psychology or the philosophy of religion. Social and behavioral scientists study the phenomenology of religion, taking a disinterested look at beliefs and practices to see what members of various groups are saying and doing. In theory, they investigate faith objectively as a purely human phenomenon. Philosophers of religion, again theoretically, begin without any bias and proceed to discover truth in an unfettered, empirical way.

Both these general approaches are attractive and can be helpful in sorting out particular beliefs and rituals of various faith groups. One could argue the objectivity of social, behavioral and philosophical investigators is limited at best, because no one approaches the phenomenon of religion without some history of prior reflection on the topic, not even professional scholars. Very few humans could be so unaffected by the world around them as to avoid forming opinions about questions as profound as those discussed by human religions.

Thor Is dead. (And your point is ...?)

British biblical scholar N.T. Wright observed: "Part of the challenge of history comes from allowing suspicion a proper role."[7] Yet, even in today's skeptical postmodern age, critical thinking about the past and present is far from normative. Every culture programs its children with a particular worldview that, at least initially, young people uncritically accept as the singular, correct, obvious way of living. This worldview includes everything from a shared spoken language, which shapes the way thoughts are expressed, to the type of foods people eat and the sexual behaviors that are permissible. The cultural divide can be enormous; a great rift can separate people who geographically live side by side. In the days of ancient Israel, the Hebrews stoned citizens to death for doing certain sexual acts in private; meanwhile their Canaanite neighbors were celebrating and reinforcing the divine gift of fertility by performing the same acts in public worship.

Various sources feed into this store of cultural information, first and foremost the home environment where most children spend their formative years. In the past, generation after generation of humans has lived inside the thought-compounds of their respective worldviews without ever seriously questioning its normative assumptions. In more recent times a monolithic worldview has become increasingly difficult for any culture to maintain. With widespread travel, free public education and now electronic communications on a global scale, a sociocultural group can no longer isolate itself from other ideas about the great questions of life. Even the Amish have to drive their horse-drawn buggies past billboards proclaiming getaway vacations to Las Vegas.

Young people may dismiss their heritage out of hand; however, every apostasy is invariably shaped by culture. As mentioned previously, when North American Christians reject religion, they seldom announce their disbelief in the Prophet Muhammad, the Olympian gods or the Buddha's Noble Eightfold Path. On April 8, 1966, the cover of *Time* fretted, to the horror of millions: "Is God Dead?" If the question-statement had asked, "Is Thor Dead?" Americans likely would have wondered what had happened to the Marvel Comics hero, a speculation that hardly would have shaken the foundations of Christendom. For an even starker contrast, Satanism—the ultimate in-your-face infidelity to traditional religion—could not exist without the Christian mythos to reject. Thinking themselves fiercely anti-Christian, Satanists turn Christian doctrine and ritual upside down and inside out, paying unintended homage to a heritage that inexorably shapes their mutiny.[8]

Embedded and Deliberative Theology

Unlike students of the phenomenology or philosophy of religion, theologians must confess their starting point within a circle of faith if they would function with integrity. On this score, I recommend an essential text for all students of religious ideas: *How to Think Theologically* by Howard Stone and James O. Duke. Stone and Duke identify two categories of theological thinking, one involving *content* and the other *process*.[9] They call these two categories of thought *embedded* and *deliberative* theology.

Ideas that people receive during youth and education combine to form an *embedded* theology. Sometimes these are so deeply rooted one is unaware of their existence. For example, when reading the words *Jesus Christ*, a series of links form in your mind, depending on what you have learned about the subject. The mental picture that emerges will depend on who you are and where you acquired the values and ideas that form your "Jesus Christ" concept, and this will affect how you look at traditional and new ideas. A Russian Orthodox priest, reading a chapter from the Gospel of Mark in his study on a frozen Moscow morning, will not reach the same conclusions about Jesus Christ as a Mormon missionary who reads the same passage under a palm tree at sunset on a Pacific island. Both are attempting to be as objective as they can be, but of course neither of them truly is. The most objective approach theology can take is to admit the truth: No one ever is totally objective. Anyone who claims otherwise is either dissembling or self-delusional.

Deliberative theology is simply the use of reason and intuitive insight to reflect on theological ideas. To do deliberative theology, creative thinkers begin with ideas about which there may be pre-existing networks of unexamined assumptions (embedded theology). Would-be theologians must learn to ask critical questions and make comparisons, requiring any free-riding concept pay its way. The best way to explain these two terms, *embedded* and *deliberative theology*, is to show them in action. So let's do that by looking at an idea introduced earlier: the difference between philosophy of religion and theological studies.

Here's a mundane example: Two people are attending a baseball game at Yankee Stadium in New York. One is a disinterested visitor from another city; the other is a lifelong Yankees fan. Both can analyze the way the game is played and in fact quite pointedly criticize the Yankees manager's strategy, but the hometown spectator operates within the circle of fans. She passionately supports the Yankees, even while decrying the foolishness of trying to steal home with two out in the ninth. Her love for the Yanks was deeply embedded by a lifetime of experiences as a New

Yorker, so that she assumes rather than contemplates her feelings about the boys in the pinstriped uniforms.

The observer from another town is more like a philosopher of religion: interested in the "game" (baseball or religious studies) but uncommitted to any team (religious viewpoint) in the fracas. In fact, baseball provides a good analogy for the theological method because, like theology, the game has both rules and options. Major League Baseball is played on a diamond-shaped field with the proper equipment. If a batter carries his tennis racket or hockey stick to the plate, he won't get to use it. Given the limitations of the game, every batter, pitcher and fielder nevertheless has a vast array of choices about how to play—hit, bunt or take the pitch; play the infield deep or in close; throw with blazing heat or confuse the batter with a floating change-up pitch. Whether a runner tries to steal second base or lingers close to the first base bag, he can't run across the diamond, tackle the pitcher and make him drop the ball. In another sport, football, players may tackle the guy with the ball, but swinging a wooden bat will get you thrown out of the game, if not arrested on the spot. The rules of a sport define the playing area and give players freedom to develop their abilities.

At first blush, the cool detachment of philosophy seems the better path, especially for skeptical postmodern people who have been bruised by zealots. Looking at religious systems through the above, admittedly contrived, sporting analogy suggests that every player operates within the confines of a worldview which is both inherited and chosen. If a Hindu theologian studies the beliefs of Islam, she does her work as a Hindu scholar and reflects on the teachings of Muhammad from her perspective as a partisan of the Hindu community. To do otherwise is intellectually dishonest, the equivalent of carrying a hockey stick onto a tennis court. Announcers and sports commentators are more like philosophers; they may critique an array of athletic contests, from basketball to water polo, with some degree of detachment, because they are not players engaged in the sport. Christians do Christianity; Hindus do Hinduism; Muslims do Islam. If that Hindu scholar ceases to look at other religions as a Hindu, she has moved from the practice of her faith to a neutral place where she is uncommitted to any point of view. As a theologian, I am skeptical that such objectivity can be achieved, although philosophers of religion assure me they can get there by paying the price of agnosticism.

Humans are inescapably shaped by the world in which they live. Here again, an embedded theology resurfaces, representing the heritage of religious ideas inherited almost without effort, shaping an unspoken, unexamined belief system. Reflecting on the difference between theology and philosophy of religion was an example of *deliberative theology*, which includes the process of comparing and contrasting different points of view to arrive at the most satisfactory conclusions about "the Divine, God and Ultimate Concerns"[10] that limited human minds can achieve.

Correlating From the Four Sources

Taking it as a given that no one approaches the study of religion empty-handed, the next question is, What tools does the aspiring theologian bring to this deliberative workshop? And are they dull or keen edged? Good theology acknowledges its beginning point, the friendly bias that comes from confident belief, and works from this starting point, attempting to correlate (Tillich's term) ideas about God (*theo-logos*) with the work of other theologians and writers who have considered the problem currently under discussion.

Before attempting this process, it is important to look at a few more basic tools, especially to review the fourfold process known popularly as the Methodist Quadrilateral, sometimes named the

Wesleyan Quadrilateral after the father of Methodism, John Wesley. This simple, effective tool, recommended by Stone and Duke, is also a system I discussed at length in two other books, *Friends in High Places* and *Glimpses of Truth*. The Quadrilateral provides a simple formula to establish dialogue among four formative factors: *Scripture, Tradition, Experience* and *Reason*. I call these the "Fantastic Four," and join Stone and Duke in shamelessly admitting to have borrowed the basic idea from the *Book of Discipline* of the United Methodist Church.[11] More recently, I have been promoting the idea of Scripture, Tradition, Experience and *Reflection*, the latter category divided into intuitive insight and intellectual analysis. I call this adaptation the Unity Quadrilateral, because it unites the thinking and feeling natures of humanity in the process of spiritual reflection.

Think of the Quadrilateral as a way of processing any religious or spiritual idea. Simply feed the concept into this handy theologizing machine and see what kind of insights you can achieve with your head and heart. The four parts are as follows:

1) *Scripture*—What did the authors of the foundational documents of the faith say to their target audiences, and what does that mean today?

2) *Tradition*—What have others thought about this, and how has it been incorporated into the life of the Church?

3) *Experience*—What have the events of my life and relationships taught me about this; what has science (including the social sciences) taught me about the world?

4) *Reflection*—As mentioned above, in my earlier books I used the exact terms of the Quadrilateral. Now I am persuaded that the last category is better expressed by the word *reflection* rather than *reason*, because theological thinking has a dual dimension, intellectual/rational and intuitive/inspirational.

a) Intellectual Reasoning. What sense can I make of this by thinking it through logically and requiring it to remain consistent with other knowledge?

b) Intuitive Reflection. What imaginative insights come to me as I let these ideas play in my mind?[12]

Assuming the Bible contains a wealth of wisdom and truth, which is a reasonable deduction when considering its positive influence through the centuries, one must nevertheless decide how to interpret the words of Scripture to access those treasures. The first factor that comes into play when reading the Bible is the **Scripture** itself—the plain sense of the text. The passage or book had to be copied and recopied, edited and translated. Next is the whole history of how people have read and understood the passage (**Tradition**). People also bring personal, cultural and societal **Experience** to the reading of biblical texts. Finally, humans apply their power to think, to **Reflect** both critically and creatively, which includes both intellectual reflection and intuitive vision. This fourfold process can help with more than just biblical texts. One can use Scripture-Tradition-Experience-Reason when mulling over any religious, sociopolitical, interpersonal or ethical concern. More immediately, as a person attempts to locate the authentic Jesus in the contradictory and sometimes unpleasant gallery of the Gospels, the "Fantastic Four" can provide some handy tools.

Every image of Jesus drawn from the Second Testament must face the fourfold test. Is it really in the Scripture text or just a cliché that interpreters have superimposed on the words? Asking what others have said, written or done about Jesus in the past helps people to understand better today. The interaction of Scripture and historical reflection on its words brings the second factor to bear, *tradition.*

Christian churches share a rich tradition of biblical and theological reflection going back to the earliest days of the faith, and it is a pluralistic tradition that speaks with a multitude of voices. For example, the tradition of mysticism insists that God can be known directly. One such form is Christian monism, which recognizes only One Presence/One Power in the cosmos. Add to this a belief in spiritual evolution, which discovers this Presence and Power at work within every sentient being to transform human consciousness into Christ consciousness, and the result is a creative process that moves from Divine Mind to a self-perfecting expression in sentient beings like humans. This is effectively summarized by Charles Fillmore as Twelve Powers, the spiritual-mental centers from which flow gifts such as *order, zeal, strength, power* and *love.*

Naturally, looking at Jesus of Nazareth through the lens of One Presence/One Power means applying principles like these to any interpretation of his nature and person. Yet anyone applying these concepts—even something as fundamental as OP^2 itself—must dialogue with the evidence presented in Christian Scripture as reflected upon by centuries of sincere, God-seeking people. Like any form of "the Way" that has come down to us since Jesus walked this earth, a practical, postmodern understanding of Christianity cannot simply invent new religious principles and call them Christian without sacrificing its intellectual and spiritual integrity.

All who identify with Jesus Christ must allow both Scripture and Christian tradition to speak their mind and heart, allowing the writers and thinkers of the past to declare truths authentically in the context in which they were created. Only after the voices from the past are given their due can Christian theology today apply new insights from its reflection upon the ancient faith. This is not an appeal for uncritical acceptance of Scripture and tradition; it is an appeal for clarity, for taking the past seriously enough to hear what others actually have said when formulating contemporary theology.

And He Walks With Me ...

The quest for a new, interactive Christology for a space-faring age does not begin in some abstract, unattainable realm of pure objectivity; it starts within the circle of Christian thought, influenced by the assumptions that each person brings to the discussion. When considering the goals of this volume, it was never my intention to produce a devotional work that merely rehearses the many attributes assigned to Jesus Christ through the ages but to look deliberatively at dominant, embedded theologies about the historical Jesus and the church-manufactured Christ of faith. If I am successful, this work should provoke a lively debate within several Christian traditions and perhaps raise a few eyebrows in the wider, theological world as well.

Countless writers and thinkers have sought a better understanding of who Jesus was and what his life and teachings mean, and each generation joins the quest. When I reflect on my first steps along this journey, a fuzzy image arises in memory, and the words of a hymn rise from the depths of my memory. It was a warm spring morning in Pennsylvania when a German Reformed Congregation rose to sing words that sounded like an invitation to fellowship with the greatest Friend a small boy could ever have.

> And He walks with me,
> And He talks with me,
> And He tells me I am His own,
> And the joy we share as we tarry there
> None other has ever known.[13]

With this sense of profound gratitude and love for Jesus of Nazareth, Christians of diverse traditions continue the age-old search by looking for a Jesus-the-Christ who can speak effectively to the space-faring, postmodern, information age of the 21st century. This interactive Jesus—the Master and Lord who walks with us and talks with us—will continue to engage humanity in the ongoing dialogue about the meaning of life and the call to higher consciousness throughout the ages to come.

To continue installing the Jesus 2.1 upgrade, please turn the page …

Jesus and the Christ: The New Paradigm

Almost immediately after Yeshua Ben Josef marched into the city of Jerusalem from the Galilean countryside of his youth, people high and low apparently began to argue about his identity. Like people everywhere who are exposed to a new phenomenon, they probably wanted to integrate this fresh prophetic figure into their worldview. The palpable tension in the questions of Pharisees and Scribes suggests they were seeking more than their own peace of mind. The whole community wanted to know his identity, mission and authority:

> Who was this man?
> What did he expect to accomplish?
> What was he teaching?
> Did he have some kind of Divine commission?
> What was his relationship to the God of Israel?

Not everybody knew about the events of his passion and death. It was, after all, a minor execution in a long train of Jew-bearing Roman crosses. Those who knew the passion story—either personally or more likely by popular rumor—would add a deeper conundrum to their litany, complicated beyond imagination by the controversial post-resurrection encounters with Jesus that his followers reported. Aroused by these dramatic events, people began to ask another question, probably with some indignation:

If God was with him, why did die so ignominiously?

This debate about the nature and person of Jesus would consume much of the energy of the young church during the first centuries of its existence. Closely related to the above questions about the prophetic activities of the living Jesus were considerations about what the Jesus Event meant now that he was safely dead:

> What did he achieve during his life?
> What did he accomplish with his death?

These concerns had deep theological, philosophical, and even political and socioeconomic ramifications, and the difficulties raised by the quest to understand the Jesus Event were so entangled that solving any one part of the equation would mean reworking the mental math in all aspects of the problem. Not surprisingly, believers often arrived at radically different answers.

Power of a Worldview

Paradoxically, the more successfully an embedded worldview defines reality for someone, the less likely the individual will be aware of its influence. Like a fish in the ocean, we swim inside a system of thought that we naturally accept as natural, ordinary, true, usually without giving much thought to alternatives. For example, most Americans are not aware of the linguistic differences in the world because we swim in a sea of English. Canadians, on the other hand, have two national languages, English and French. Unless an American lives in a place with high concentrations of non-English speakers, the likelihood of giving any thought to the diversity of human languages in the course of a normal work day in the USA is very slim. It is also possible to drive hundreds of miles in the USA without crossing state lines, so Americans are not even consciously aware of political boundaries. This linguistic expectation permeates American thinking, so much that starship crews in Gene Roddenberry's *Star*

Trek universe always seemed unfazed whenever they discovered aliens who effortlessly spoke American English on planets scattered across the galaxy.

Not so for Europeans, who are more alert to the multilingual nature of the human family because of the proximity of language groups to each other. Traveling a few hundred miles in Europe can take you across three countries and several language families. Switzerland alone has four national languages: French, German, Italian and the lesser known regional language, Romansh. My daughter-in-law, Kinga Schlesinger, is a Polish citizen who has worked as an interpreter for the European Union. Kinga speaks Russian, German, French, English, and, of course, Polish. Although her achievements are stellar by U.S. standards, her fluency in multiple languages is not uncommon for Europeans.

When I was a soldier stationed in Germany back in the 1960s, I was conversing on a street corner with a young German I'd just met. Mercifully for me, he spoke English, because my conversational German is minimal. As we talked a youth with a backpack approached and asked directions to the Franco-German border, in French, of course. My new German friend replied in that language, then translated for me. For the next few minutes, this native German speaker hopped back and forth between English and French rather effortlessly.

As he switched languages I had one of those *ah-ha!* moments— an epiphany of the obvious, the kind that today I punctuate with a mental slap of the forehead and silent version of Homer Simpson's "Doh!" My brilliant ratiocination? English isn't spoken everywhere by everyone! Sure, I knew intellectually that humans communicate in a multitude of languages; I'd studied Latin and Spanish in high school, and I'd read that Africa alone has over 2,000 distinct languages. Yet I had never previously ventured outside the sea of spoken English. The multilingual nature of this planet seized me in an instant; I felt like a fish, wave-tossed onto the beach, gasping for air in a new, incomprehensible world, and a new paradigm of human communication came alive:

Hosanna!
English isn't spoken by everyone!
People think with different words ...
   Arranged
     in
        different
           patterns.
And since the vocabulary and writing system and
structure of language
  Shape_the_Way_Thoughts_are_Formed,
People naturally and necessarily think differently,
  and always
have. Differently thought.
Differences are predictably NormaL.

If such myopia is possible about something as obvious as the language I speak, how much more confusion might exist when considering religious ideas? What assumptions am I making about the nature of Ultimate Reality, which people from disparate religio-cultural backgrounds might abjure?

Conflicting Paradigms

Church history has provided a wide spectrum of answers to the basic questions of the nature, person and work of Jesus Christ. Nevertheless, people today are so accustomed to radio and TV evangelists invoking a particular view of Jesus' nature and work—i.e., fully God and fully human, two natures with one will, whose death at Calvary paid the price for the sins of all those who freely accept him as Lord and Savior—that most Christians are blithely ignorant of the origins of this comparatively modern interpretation of the Jesus Event. In his book *The Heart of Christianity*, biblical scholar Marcus J. Borg points to a dichotomy in Christian thought today, an old paradigm of divine, inerrant literalism, juxtaposed against an emerging new paradigm that sees the Bible as an anthology of ancient wisdom. The amazing fact is that, although it contains elements which are quite ancient, the "old" paradigm is of relatively recent origin. Borg writes:

> For the past few centuries, this earlier way of see-
> ing Christianity, what I call an "earlier para-
> digm," has been shared in common by most
> Christians in Western culture. It remains a major
> voice in North American Christianity ... this ear-
> lier way of being Christian views the Bible as the
> unique revelation of God, emphasizes its literal
> meaning, and sees the Christian life as centered
> in believing now for the sake of salvation later—
> typically, believing in God, the Bible, and Jesus as
> the way to heaven. Typically, it has also seen
> Christianity as the only true religion.[1]

Borg emphasizes that the "old" paradigm is not a doctrine of the early church but a much newer construction. For example, taking the Bible as an inerrant, infallible document is hardly an ancient concept. That kind of narrow Biblicism first appeared in the 17th century and wasn't widely accepted until the 19th and 20th centuries. Borg offers a new look at the faith of Jesus:

> The second way of seeing Christianity, the
> "emerging paradigm," has been developing for
> over a hundred years and has recently become a
> major grassroots movement within mainline
> denominations. Positively, it is the product of
> Christianity's encounter with the modern and
> postmodern world, including science, historical

> scholarship, religious pluralism, and cultural
> diversity. Less positively, it is the product of our
> awareness of how Christianity has contributed to
> racism, sexism, nationalism, exclusivism, and
> other harmful ideologies.[2]

Borg makes an important point about another, much older paradigm, i.e., the tendency to define the Christian faith as a set of beliefs about ideas. This earlier paradigm holds that faith is intellectually concurring to a series of statements, often about quasi-historical events or theological doctrines. For example, if you believe in traditional doctrines like the Virgin Birth, the Second Coming and the inerrancy of the Bible, then you have faith. Conversely, if you can't get aboard the particular train of facts that your church or denomination requires, you have little or no faith. Since the definition of faith is affirming the truth of certain facts, it follows that questioning those facts is lack of faith. To view the facts differently is not merely wrong; it is the very definition of disbelief and evil. When the content of those required beliefs is supplied by Protestant fundamentalism, the results are predictable.

Getting the facts right is essential to the old paradigm, so discussions about faith quickly deteriorate into disputes over specific points of doctrine, the historicity of the Bible, and other ideas that a person is required to affirm in order to be a Christian. Faith for the old paradigm means giving mental assent to a list of beliefs, which Borg describes with the Latin word *assensus*.[3]

Faith as *Assensus* (i.e., Assent)

The old paradigm defined faith in terms of belief. You have faith if you believe certain facts about Jesus, the Bible, God and salvation. Sometimes the facts-based formula provided explicit guidance, e.g., the Athanasian Creed, ca. 500 CE: "He therefore that will be saved must thus think of the Trinity."[4] Mere adoration of the Trinity was insufficient; to achieve salvation, people had to believe in the Trinity in a strictly specified way ("thus think"). In the old paradigm, salvation occurs at the point in time when a person is convinced to "thus think" about points of doctrine and the events of church history.

To have faith is to accept certain facts, and fundamentalist Christianity is one of the most adamantly facts-based religions in history. The World Congress of Fundamentalists, meeting in 1976, defined Christian fundamentalism as the faith that

> ... affirms the foundational truths of the historic Christian Faith: The doctrine of the Trinity; the incarnation, virgin birth, substitutionary atonement, bodily resurrection and glorious ascension, and Second Coming of the Lord Jesus Christ; the new birth through regeneration by the Holy Spirit; the resurrection of the saints to life eternal; the resurrection of the ungodly to final judgment and eternal death; the fellowship of the saints, who are the body of Christ.[5]

Notice the list is entirely cognitive. A believer must "affirm the foundational truths of the historic Christian faith," which are all *ideas*. Not a word in here about behavior—no injunction to do anything about clothing the naked or feeding the hungry; no requirement to pray, or practice kindness, or celebrate the love of God with others. Not even the ceremonial need to practice rituals of remembrance, like the Eucharist or Christian baptism. Faith in the old paradigm is assent to ideas, facts and doctrines, which means evolutionary change in religious thinking is unthinkable. *God said it ... that settles it.* This worldview makes the faith of Jesus as intractable as the flat earth, with little chance for dialogue or growth.

Faith in Jesus Christ under the old paradigm is assent to the *facts* of Jesus' birth, life, death, resurrection-experience and the post-resurrection appearance of the risen Lord. If people cannot bring themselves to accept the historicity of all the events—i.e., Jesus' virgin birth, bodily resurrection and literal second coming—then they are denying faith in Jesus Christ, precisely because faith meant belief in facts.

Biblical scholar and historian Elaine Pagels says this emphasis on intellectual assent has been blown way out of proportion in contemporary Christian thought. "Beliefs are overrated in Christianity, Pagels writes. "Religious traditions have to do with a lot more than beliefs."[6]

Nothing like these mental gymnastics was ever required by Jesus during his earthly ministry. In fact, Jesus explicitly rejected the faith-as-facts model. When he was asked point-blank by a student of the Torah, "What must I do to inherit eternal life?" Jesus replied like any good rabbi, with a gentle touch that emphasized love and the ethical elements of the Jewish Law. He told the man to love the Lord with all his heart, soul, strength and mind; and to love his neighbor as much as he loved himself, then added, "Do this, and you will live."[7] Not a word about proper belief formulas or facts he must accept. Centuries later the high councils, which declared official Christian doctrines, apparently never considered the opposing view of Jesus as recorded in the Second Testament. Faith had become the doctrine of mental assent, *assensus*.

Faced with this ultimatum, countless thoughtful people through the ages have rejected both the Bible and Jesus. Faith as *assensus* especially alienates modern people by demanding they affirm a prescientific worldview: The earth was created in six days; there was no evolution because all humanity descended from a literal Adam and Eve; a great flood destroyed all life not spared in Noah's Ark; language differences come from the Tower of Babel; snakes, trees and donkeys talk; genocide in warfare is acceptable if commanded by God; slaves must obey their masters; God needed the blood of Jesus to deal with His anger management problem; Jesus will return in the clouds of the sky.

The earlier paradigm has made vivid mythology and good poetry into inaccurate history and bad science. Furthermore, the faith-as-facts model actually turns its back on key biblical teachings. According to the Gospels, Jesus was less concerned with the specifics about what people believed than he was about how their God-consciousness demonstrated itself through acts of compassion. The early Church seemed to agree. For example, compare the faith-as-assensus doctrine with the following passages from the scrappy Letter of James:

> My friends, what good is it for one of you to say that you have faith if your actions do not prove it? Can that faith save you? Suppose there are brothers or sisters who need clothes and don't have enough to eat. What good is there in your saying to them, "God bless you! Keep warm and eat well!"—if you don't give them the necessities of life? So it is with faith: if it is alone and includes no actions, then it is dead. But someone will say, "One person has faith, another has actions." My answer is, "Show me how anyone can have faith without actions. I will show you my faith by my actions."[8]

James even invokes first-century folklore to drive home his point. If faith is *assensus*, merely believing certain facts are true, doesn't that mean evil spirits have faith?

> Do you believe that there is only one God? Good! The demons also believe—and tremble with fear.[9]

One does not have to believe in evil spirits to see where James is going. "Demons are hardly model Christians," James is saying. "Yet these bad guys believe in God. In fact, they believe it so strongly it scares them witless!" Although he wrapped it in mythological symbolism, James is clearly arguing that simple intellectual assent cannot be the basic ingredient. Faith as *assensus* substitutes doctrinal accuracy for the radical freedom offered by Jesus. Marcus J. Borg suggests there are other options. For people of the emerging paradigm, faith is not *assensus* (assent) to a series of propositions, but a combination of *feducia* (trust), *fidelitas* (faithfulness or fidelity), and *visio* (vision, seeing the whole).[10]

Faith as *Feducia* (i.e., *Trust*)

To define faith with the Latin word *feducia,* or *trust,* brings the discussion to a new level. Faith as *feducia* describes belief as the manner in which someone responds to life. Do I trust God, regardless of circumstances or appearances? Am I willing to "let go and let God," to turn my deepest concerns over to the Divine Power and Presence that animates the cosmos, and love God regardless of the outcome? Borg compares *feducia* to floating on a vast, deep ocean. When I struggle, taking my attention off God, I sink like Peter did when he let himself be distracted from focusing on the Divine Presence. Relaxing, I will float. Faith-as-trust is relaxing into God, a marvelous, calming image, taught by most of the great religions of humanity.

The opposite of faith-as-trust is not disbelief but *mistrust.* "More interestingly and provocatively," Borg adds, "its opposite is 'anxiety' or 'worry.'" When Jesus fishes Peter from the sea after the fisherman's botched attempt at walking on water, the Master chides him with the words, "You of little faith, why did you doubt?" The mythological nature of this story notwithstanding, it is clear from the context that Jesus was not asking Peter to affirm a set of beliefs but to trust that God's power would keep him safe.[11]

Feducia requires no mental gamesmanship, no assent to a set of facts or doctrines. It is the experience of sitting alone in a house of worship, or looking up at the starry night sky, and simply realizing that God has everything under control. Faith as *feducia* reaches beyond intellectual mastery of theological principles to an experience of ultimate trust in God.

Faith as *Fidelitas* (i.e., Faithfulness or Fidelity)

Faith can also be understood as *fidelitas*, which Borg translates "faithfulness," or "fidelity." Faith-as-fidelity does not mean allegiance to statements *about* God, written or otherwise; *fidelitas* is faithfulness *to* God, the kind of loyalty and connection experienced in committed human relationships. "*Fidelitas* refers to a radical centering in God."[12]

As in human relationships, the opposite of *fidelitas* is not disbelief but *infidelity*. Biblically, the metaphors of Israel as unfaithful lover, adulteress and idolater all come from prophetic judgments upon their generation's infidelity to God. The book of Hosea presents an ongoing allegory about Israel as a harlot whom God nevertheless loves, regardless of how unfaithful the people have been. Later, in the Gospels, Jesus rejects the demand from skeptical Pharisees for a magical, validating sign from heaven by calling them "an evil and adulterous generation."[13] It is highly unlikely that Jesus was talking about the salacious sexual behavior of Jewish Torah scholars here; instead, like the classical prophets had done, he selected the metaphor of infidelity to summon his contemporaries to self-examination about their fidelity to God.

Faith as *Visio* (i.e., Vision, Seeing the Whole)

All four Gospel writers offer different pictures of Jesus, so that it is usually better to speak of "Matthew's Jesus" and "John's Jesus" to differentiate the literary characters confronting the reader in each work. The four evangelists are unanimous in presenting Jesus as someone whose agenda is radically different from everyone else in his world. The Gospels frequently illustrate how difficult it was for Jesus to get his concept of the Kingdom of Heaven across to people, even those who were close to him. When it comes to comprehending the message of Jesus, the disciples are often portrayed rather unflatteringly; in fact, in several places they come across as clueless dullards.

According to Luke, writing in the Acts of the Apostles, the colossal disconnect between what Jesus taught and what they understood prevailed to the end of Jesus' ministry on earth. The last question the disciples asked before Jesus ascended into heaven is, "Lord, is this the time when you will restore the kingdom to Israel?"[14] Luke's dialogue is a caricature of an oblivious first generation Church that *still* hasn't gotten the message, even after the ascension of the Lord!

Jesus offered more than faith-as-trust and faith-as-fidelity; his life presented people with a new way of looking at the world. Borg describes this spiritually enhanced worldview with the Latin word *visio,* meaning *vision,* or *seeing the whole.* It is very like the word *gestalt,* which refers to separate pieces coming together to form a new vision of the whole.[15] *Visio* is the *ah-ha!* experience, when unrelated pieces suddenly relate, and a new picture emerges. It is worldview, life orientation, unspoken assumptions and the paradigm itself. Faith-as-vision asks, "What are your unspoken assumptions about the nature of life itself? Do you feel life is hostile, indifferent or nurturing?" *Visio* expects people to choose the latter if they would be followers of Jesus.[16]

The man of Nazareth experienced life as supportive, *gracious,* even though his path led to the cross. His self-sacrifice can only be understood as a supreme act of faith in the goodness of God, the worthiness of humanity, and the ultimate triumph of love over hate. The opposite of faith as vision is not disbelief but narrow-mindedness.

Marcus J. Borg's concept of old and emerging paradigms in the Western world appears to have merit in helping postmodern Christianity understand its place in the new constellation of human religious groups in the 21st century.

The Vantage Point of History

It is my conviction that the rise of a destructive fundamentalism in Christianity, Islam and Judaism as well as among the religions of the East is a necessary phase through which all of us must go before we break out of our limited religious boxes to embrace a new consciousness. Those threatened by the future that they cannot yet embrace have retreated into the religious certainties of the past. That is almost always a prelude to a new breakthrough.[1]

—Bishop John Shelby Spong

Thinking about the Jesus of history is somewhat like looking at a constellation in the evening sky. The Big Dipper, or as the ancients called it, *Ursa Major*, the Great Bear, only appears dipper-like from the surface of Earth, and even then it is only visible in the Northern Hemisphere. The light forming the Dipper left those stars hundreds or even thousands of years ago, so gazing into the heavens actually means looking back in time. More than that, human history complicates the way people look at *Ursa Major*. Images come to mind. Sailors watching the sky for a clearing in the clouds to spot the Big Dipper for locating the North Star at the handle of its smaller companion, *Ursa Minor*. Slaves escapimg northward along the Underground Railway with the lyrics of "Follow the Drinking Gourd" guiding their steps in the night.

The Big Dipper isn't just a string of lights in a dark sky. History has shaped the Great Bear.

How much more has 2,000 years of human experience shaped the way we look at Jesus Christ? Thinking about the founder of the Christian faith is like peering backward through time, but the distance between the present time and his era—from Yeshua Ben Josef, the unlettered rebel who overturned the ancient world as he upended the tables of the money changers, to 21st-century Christians, who peck at their laptops to order stocks from an online broker thousands of miles away—is hardly a straight shot through the vacuum of space. The thought-debris of centuries clutters the gap between him and postmodern humanity: layers of interpretation, violent reactions against "heresies" and their purveyors; powerful personalities who have shaped the way people look at Jesus; the struggle of movements and countermovements; world events, politics and socioeconomic influences; tribalism, nationalism and emerging internationalism; linguistic, cultural and ethnic factors; education, geography, social class, race, gender, sexual orientation—oh, yes, and religious beliefs too.

Swedish Jesus Makes House Calls

Language and culture powerfully influence worldview. Social and linguistic factors interplay to form systems of thought and behavior that influence the way people look at the prophet from Nazareth. During my initial studies for the ministry at Lancaster Theological Seminary, I was loitering between classes near a large copy of a painting of Jesus. Although the decades-old memory is fuzzy, I believe it may have been the famous portrait of Jesus by Warner Sallman (1892–1968), which illustrates the verse "Behold, I stand at the door and knock." In any event, many of the customary "portraits" of the Nazarene show him as a European Caucasian rather than a dark-complexioned Semite. Ordinarily, I would never have given it a thought, but this time I happened to be waiting with my best friend at seminary, an African-American student named Nathan Baxter. Although raised in the charismatic Church of God in Christ, Nate would one day become an Episcopal Priest, Dean of Lancaster Seminary, and Dean of the National Cathedral in Washington, D.C. At present, he serves as Bishop of the Episcopal Diocese of Central Pennsylvania in my native state, and I sometimes quip that if the Catholic and Episcopal churches ever reunite, he'll be on the short list for Pope. All this glory was still in the future when we 20-something seminary students stood beneath that blonde-haired, fair-skinned portrait of the Savior.

The future Bishop Nate swept the painting with an icy glance and grumbled, "Look at that. Jesus was a Swede."

He was absolutely right. When Sallman painted his illustration of the well-known biblical text—which ever since I have been irreverently calling "The Swedish Jesus Makes House Calls"—the artist was doing what everyone does, i.e., creating Jesus in his own image. Sallman was a European-American. Seeing Jesus as an interactive figure makes this process more understandable, but the obligation incurred by awareness of this process requires continuous self-corrective measures to remind myself that the Jesus I see is not the only Jesus possible.

Ethnocentrism Unavoidable: Rap Music and the Generation Gap

Every group, whether defined by ethnicity, language, race, religion or a combination of factors, sees the world through its own cultural window, and some degree of ethnocentrism is unavoidable. People grow up in a social structure they did not create, biologically hard-wired to accept the worldview of their cultural pool, more or less without question. How can an infant do otherwise? It's not as though a baby born in Damascus can decide to grow up speaking Urdu and practicing the Hindu faith. Children accept whatever cultural environment they inherit as the natural, normal and proper way of living. Some people may find this naive plasticity hard to recognize, especially if they have raised a rebellious teenager. Even young people raised in free-thinking Western civilization will seldom toss aside knife and fork to eat everyday food with chopsticks, unless the family is ethnically Asian and attempting to preserve their cultural heritage.

Young people today are a good example. Regardless of their racial/ethnic background, millions of youth love listening to rap music—which to me sounds less like music and more like a cross between a skipping phonograph record and a major league manager having a fistfight with the home plate umpire. While my kids rejected the normative, melodious music of their parents' generation (such as Johnny Mathis, Billy Joel, Dan Fogelberg, John Denver—I could go on, but you get the point), they never considered rejecting the capitalist infrastructure and technology of the electronic media that piped those hyperactive, screeching-blackboard-chalk, nonmusical discordant sounds to them.

Of course, my evaluation of rap is perfectly objective and theirs is biased toward the youth culture, but if you are old enough to have a tinge of grey hair you already know this. Kids are wrapped in their musical world as surely as their parents are wrapped in theirs, and the two planets almost never share a common orbit. In fact, one of my secret beliefs is that young people select music expressly designed to drive their parents batty. (My baby boomer crowd assailed our WWII-generation parents with Elvis, and later the Beatles.)

The nature of a rebellion is shaped by the very culture against which dissatisfied parties stage their revolt. When British-American colonists dumped tea into Boston Harbor in 1773, it was because they felt that King George had violated their rights as Englishmen. The Declaration of Independence, penned two years later, was grounded in English Common Law and made no reference to the Code of Bushido, which at that time guided life in feudal Japan, or the Sharia, Islamic Law, which governed the Muslim world. Should it then be surprising that a pastor of an all-black Holiness church in rural Mississippi looks at Jesus differently than an Irish-American Catholic nun who teaches at a parochial school in New York City? Is it hard to imagine that a professor of Second Testament Studies at a liberal Protestant bastion like Harvard Divinity School or New York City's Union Theological Seminary will look at Jesus differently than a professor teaching the same academic discipline at ultraconservative institutions like Liberty Baptist University or Bob Jones University?

The Believers in It

If the specific gravity of a subject makes objectivity difficult, how much more with topics of Ultimate Concern? For some people, the very foundations of the universe tremble at any suggestion of alternative ways to look at Jesus, and consequently the notion of an interactive Jesus is both terrifying and blasphemous to them. The familiar, blunt declaration seen on bumper stickers summarizes this need for uncritical certainty: "God said it, I believe it, and that settles it!" The niggling difficulty in this affirmation—which is based on the old paradigm of faith as mental assent to certain facts—centers on how to find definite faith in the indefinite pronoun "it." Whenever I see this message on the back of a car, I am tempted to roll down my window and ask, "What's the 'it' that God said and you believe?"

At the risk of running away on a Clintonesque tangent, the manner in which those bumper stickers abuse the word *it* needs to be addressed, because it covers a multitude of intellectual sins. If the "it" that must be obediently believed is the Bible, then some discussion about verb tenses is required when thinking about the Scripture:

1) Simple past—what "it" *meant* to the people for whom "it" was written.

2) Present Perfect—what "it" *has meant* through the centuries during an ongoing evolution in intellectual, social and political institutions.

3) Present—what "it" *means* today in the 21st century.

4) Future—what "it" *will mean* as humanity moves out into the cosmos and encounters other sentient life forms.

Gall in the Family

Discussing religious topics objectively remains a challenge in this scientific age, partly because theological questions are seldom considered outside a narrow safety zone of think-alikes, but more often because of the cultural and intellectual gulf between old and new paradigms. Not just differences, but outright hostility seems to prevail. Social scientists might point out that, like Hinduism, Christianity is not so much a religion but a family of religions. If so, there has been little dialogue among the warring branches of the Christian family, which would be judged dysfunctional by any reasonable standard.

Because of all these factors, I am under no illusion that any work such as this one—which 1) proceeds from a set of assumptions grounded in a "metaphysical" understanding of Christianity, 2) attempts to correlate contemporary experience with scholarship from the social and behavioral sciences, and 3) offers new theological paradigms about some of the most fundamental components of the Christian worldview—will be warmly received in all the subcircles of the family faith. I am hopeful that those who are open to new discussion of Christological questions—usually the cultural creatives, liberals and progressive moderates of assorted stripes and persuasions—will consider the efficacy of these ideas and recognize the Practical Christian perspective that informs them as a valid continuation of the mystical-Transcendentalist tradition within Christian thought.

To prepare a space age paradigm for the Jesus Event first requires another look at the ancient discussion and review of other models that have influenced Christian thought over time. Having considered the preprogrammed difficulties every theologian faces when approaching a study of Christology, the discussion now turns to the various solutions the early church devised to answer the crucial questions about Jesus Christ. Looking backward is absolutely essential, a process to approach eagerly, because interacting with the Jesus models of antiquity can help people learn how to love their neighbors and themselves better today.

- 8 -

The Apostles

Earliest Attempts to Make Sense of the Jesus Event

When the men had come to him, they said, "John the Baptist has sent us to you to ask, 'Are you the one who is to come, or are we to wait for another?'"

—Luke 7:20

"Christos"—The Anointed One

Along with its complex theology, the Apostles' Creed—which was probably not written by the Apostles but developed a few generations later—describes an historic event in stark, simple words: *Jesus Christ ... suffered under Pontius Pilate, was crucified, died and was buried.* When pondering the final scenes in the drama of Jesus' life, the primitive church realized that much more was at stake here than the death of yet another good man. If God were with him, how could Jesus have failed so miserably? The emotional-theological burden of his unanticipated demise threatened to smother the newborn Jesus movement under a heavy pillow of cognitive dissonance.

Effectively speaking, Jesus had founded a militantly nonpartisan people's party, whose members abandoned everything to follow him across the countryside in the hope of realizing a series of abstract and concrete goals, to include transforming their

Roman-dominated world into a Kingdom of God—the like of which no one had ever seen and for which they longed after millennia of "ungodly" rulers—and healing the sick and lame, whom they encountered in the streets and marketplace every day. A significant cadre of disciples who followed Yeshua Ben Josef had come to believe the humble Nazarene carpenter was the national Christ, the Anointed One, the Savior of Israel.

People today usually speak of *Christ* as if it were the second part of a personal name. Western society is accustomed to a two-name designation—John *Kennedy*, son of Joseph and Rose *Kennedy*. Although *Christ* was obviously not his family name (as in Robert W. Funk's observation about *Jesus Christ*, son of Joseph and Mary *Christ)*, this descriptive theological term has unfortunately become interchangeable with the name of the historical person.[1]

Since the Second Testament was written in Koine Greek for a Greek-speaking Hellenistic world, *Christos* was the preferred Greek translation for the First Testament Hebrew word *mashiach*, usually translated the *anointed one*.[2] You will recognize the English version of the word, *messiah*. Ancient Near Eastern kings, prophets and priests were often consecrated to their offices by a ceremonial drizzling of oil upon their heads, and so the word *mashiach* literally means "drizzled one." It was a ritual not unlike royal coronation, or the more mundane event of consecrating-ordaining a person to ministry. The practice is described frequently in First Testament texts, e.g., Samuel anointed Saul and David, respectively, as a signal of God's passing favor. The practice finds its way into the most popular Hebrew psalm: "You anoint my head with oil, my cup overflows."[3]

Belief in a heavenly messiah became a focal point in Jewish theology after the continuous failure of earthly kings in bringing about God's rule on earth. This is even more evident in the literature emerging during the Intertestamental period than in the

Hebrew Bible. When Christians began pondering the ministry of Jesus, it became obvious to some of them that the man of Nazareth fulfilled those expectations. They believed he fulfilled the prophecies of the anointed one. The idea of a messiah as a deliverer, who would raise Israel from sinful obscurity to righteousness and independence, is remarkably absent from the Hebrew Bible. Although there are a few First Testament mumblings that sound like hints of a coming messiah to Christianized ears, only in the Intertestamental literature—a hodgepodge of Greek and Aramaic texts written by Jewish apocalyptic prophets between the end of Hebrew writings in the second century BCE and beginnings of the NT Christian canon in first century CE—is there unequivocal confidence in the Messianic Hope.

The cult of *mashiach* Adventists drew its growth energy more from sociopolitical circumstances than religious sources. Like people born during slavery in 19th-century America, ancient Israel was a land where few citizens could separate religious themes from the sufferings of a subjugated people. Jewish nationalism had briefly flourished after the Maccabean revolt, which overthrew Seleucid Greek rule in the 160s BCE and re-established the Kingdom of Israel for about a century under Hasmonean rule, a term deriving from *Hashman*, the Maccabean clan name. Later successors to the throne naively invited the Romans to settle domestic political squabbles, effectively ending the independent existence of the Jewish state until its re-establishment by a vote of the United Nations after the Holocaust of World War II. Down through the centuries, whenever the Torah was read in synagogues, the grand promises God had made to Israel still cried for fulfillment. The Messiah would bring the Kingdom of God, not simply another earthly kingdom. Some Jews believe the prophecy has been fulfilled in the State of Israel. However, in one of those head-spinning contradictions that frequently characterize human religious thought, some ultraorthodox Jewish groups refuse to recognize the State of Israel precisely because Israel cannot be re-established until the Messiah comes. He's not here, so neither is Israel.[4]

Actually, this ongoing controversy is historically consistent. After the collapse of the Kingdom of Israel, multitudes of Jewish exiles living in *Diaspora* (or dispersion) at places like Babylon, Alexandria, Carthage and Rome wondered how their promised land, blessed and protected by the One True God, could cease to exist. Perhaps there would come a Deliverer, like Joshua, to lead the people back from this exile to freedom.[5] When concerns about the apparent unfairness of life and the triumph of the unrighteous were added to the mix, the Messianic Hope took on supernatural dimensions, forecasting a great Judgment Day in which the scales of justice would be balanced by the punishment of the wicked and the reward of the faithful.

"Are you he who is to come ...?"

By the time Jesus reached the Jordan River around 30 CE, itinerant preachers like John the Baptist were stirring up the people with hopes of this great, impending adjustment in the spiritual ecology of the cosmos. The late Dr. Robert W. Funk, well-known biblical scholar and guiding light of the Jesus Seminar, wrote:

> John offered a populist alternative to the temple purification process for sin. People flocked out to him in the wilderness as he announced the imminent wrath of God amidst apocalyptic fervor and expectations of divine intervention.[6]

Significantly, the Gospels show that some of Jesus' early disciples floated his way from John's overflowing pool of followers. Both Matthew and Luke report that the Baptist ordered his disciples to ask Jesus if the Nazarene were the "one who is to come" (Mt. 11:3, Lk. 7:19). The story of Jesus' baptism, recorded in all four Gospels, shows John practically leaping out of the water to greet Jesus on the shore. Assuming these narratives are fictionalized retellings of an actual historical event, what are the Gospel authors/editors saying here? Obviously, that John sent his people to meet with Jesus because John wanted them to follow the real messiah after Herod did his worst to the Baptist. The not-too-subtle message in these encounters between Jesus and the followers of John, indeed in the Jesus-John interactions as a whole, presents John and Jesus as a one-two punch, Forerunner and Messiah. The barely hidden implication of these stories is that to be faithful to the mission of the Baptist, John's followers should all flock to Jesus. After all, John himself testifies repeatedly to his insignificance and Jesus' supremacy, and Luke says John was Jesus' kinsman. When Mary visited her pregnant cousin, Elizabeth, John the fetus "leaped in her womb."[7]

This theme of John's subservience to Jesus repeats with enough regularity that one begins to suspect there was something going on here, and indeed there likely was. When the Christian Gospels were written in the last decades of the first century, followers of the beheaded Baptist still persisted in Judea. The third century Pseudo-Clementine Writings may reflect old memories when they report:

> Yea, some even of the disciples of John (the Baptist), who seemed to be great ones, have separated themselves from the people, and proclaimed their own master as the Christ.[8]

Some scholars believe the Gospel passages about John were penned almost like an ad campaign: *Okay, all you John-the-Baptist people, listen up! So, Johnnie wasn't the Messiah? No problemo. John-the-B wanted you guys to follow Jesus, because he knew Jesus was the real deal ...*

Clueless in High Places

In any event, the responses of the disciples of Jesus described in Second Testament passages suggest that several of them bought the whole messianic package and superimposed it on the mission and message of Jesus. In fact, a significant body of modern scholarship holds that Jesus never claimed to be the Messiah, much less God incarnate, but saw himself as a prophetic figure and teacher. Certainly, there are enough passages where Jesus turns aside praise and either rejects the offer or orders silent those who want to proclaim him as the Christ. Are these verses authentic sayings of Jesus? What about other Scriptures where Jesus does claim a unique relationship with the Father? The struggle to understand the Jesus Event twisted the memories of the first-century church and produced contradictory Second Testament images of him, because even in the first generation Jesus was an interactive figure whose message and mission changed depending on who was telling the story.[9]

As mentioned in Chapter 2, the book of Acts reports that the last question the disciples asked Jesus before he ascended into heaven was, "Lord, is this the time when you will restore the kingdom to Israel?"[10] One can almost hear Luke's between-the-lines message to his Hellenistic, gentile readers, who believed without ever having seen Jesus in the flesh: *How could anybody be so clueless after traveling with Jesus for three years? You wonder why all the Jews have not flocked to accept Jesus as Messiah? Look! Even his closest followers didn't get it until the Holy Spirit descended on them at Pentecost!*

Mark's Jesus takes pains to conceal any aspirations to messiahship until the last moment when Jesus is confronted by the high priest:

> Again the high priest asked him, "Are you the Messiah, the Son of the Blessed One?" Jesus said,

> "I am; and 'you will see the Son of Man seated at
> the right hand of the Power,' and 'coming with
> the clouds of heaven.'"[11]

Here the model is not a Davidic kingship to re-establish Israel but a divine consummation on the Day of Judgment, another option the subjugated people of ancient Palestine considered acceptable. When neither national liberation nor supernatural culmination came quickly, the disciples faced harsh reality. Jesus died with the Romans still in power, and the stars did not fall from the heavens. Indeed, by the time the book of Acts was written, probably in the 80s of the first century, the Church was beginning to wonder when, if ever, The End would come. From the tone of the NT writings, few people in the early generations believed the kingdom of God would have to be amortized over 2,000 years and counting.

The apparent debacle of Jesus' earthly ministry was more than a stumbling block to the small band of disciples. Reasonably speaking, a crucified messiah should have put them out of business. How could the Chosen One sent by God have failed so miserably? Didn't Moses prevail against Pharaoh, Joshua against the cities of the Canaanites, Gideon against the Midianites—*everybody* sent by God against anybody else? When Great Babylon carried the Jews into exile, did they not return to re-establish the Temple and rebuild Jerusalem's walls? The Jewish people had survived conqueror after conqueror because the Lord God had promised His chosen people He would not abandon them. No wonder prophets continually sang of a deliverer who would one day come to re-establish the independence of Israel and create his kingdom on earth. To the disciples of Yeshua Ben Josef, the Nazarene was this Promised One. So the full-time followers of Jesus must have been in shock those first days after his execution. Now that he was dead, they faced a more immediate foe than mere spiritual disillusionment. They were unemployed.

Jesus Has Left the Building ...

The followers of Jesus had to decide what his death meant to their continued allegiance to him. Could he still lead them from beyond the grave? If Jesus was sent by God, how could he have been executed alongside two common criminals? *Surely there must be some significance to his sacrifice*, they said to themselves. What could it be?

Yet the life force of Jesus—whether one considers him divine, human or some combination thereof—certainly proved stronger than death. What happened historically will never be known, but there is no doubt that soon after his execution key members of the fellowship began to report encounters with the Risen Lord. Postmodern Christians may take the Resurrection with a healthy dose of skepticism, but it was the crucifixion rather than the resurrection that caused problems for the primitive church. Apocalyptic Jews expected a general resurrection of the dead in the End Times, which they thought were upon them like every generation does, so a risen Jesus could slip into the first wave of those who were to return at the Day of Judgment.

Beyond the specific expectations of Jewish apocalyptic theology, biblical encounters between a post-resurrection Jesus and his disciples doubtless were fed by a prescientific penchant to see everyday life in supernatural terms. Demons, angels and assorted supernatural beings were part of the mental furniture of first-century Middle Eastern culture, if not the whole ancient world. Twenty centuries later, people might wonder how anyone could mistakenly believe that a popular figure had risen from the dead. They could, quite easily, especially in a world without electronic media or photography. In fact, the Jewish world forbade all forms of realistic art in the "no graven images" commandment, so handmade sketches of the man from Nazareth would not have been in circulation. Who knew what the dead person looked like, except those who had seen him up close and personal?

This makes the strange tale of the walk to Emmaus totally believable. At first, two followers of Jesus failed to recognize the Risen Lord, even though they walked with him for hours. After listening to him discourse at length on the meaning of the Scripture, they suddenly realized who this stranger was.

> Then their eyes were opened, and they recognized him; and he vanished from their sight. They said to each other, "Were not our hearts burning within us while he was talking to us on the road, while he was opening the scriptures to us?"[12]

Whatever actually happened in the days after Good Friday can be debated, but it is undeniably true that stories about the reappearance of Jesus impacted the small band of followers. Scholars might disagree about which came first. Did the stories about the Risen Lord empower the primitive church, or did the church modify and enhance those stories in support of its growing missionary efforts? In this example, did Jesus appear to two men on the road to Emmaus, or did a small group of disciples encounter a stranger who discussed the spiritual significance of recent events with them, leaving their presence to continue his journey, an event later interpreted as a vision of Jesus: *Was that the Lord?*

Still, what would lead people to believe they had seen a person whom others reported as dead? In a bizarre 20th-century replica of this phenomenon, consider the plethora of quasi-religious sightings of Elvis Presley after his death. Many of his fans refused to believe the King of Rock and Roll was gone forever. Similar energies seem to be at work among those who believe JFK survived his assassination and has been maintained on life-support machines at a super-secret location since 1963.[13] The sudden loss of a highly prized life bewilders the human psyche. Jesus could just not have died ... really died. The mind rightly rebels against it, and if people today can still feel the absurdity of Jesus' untimely death 21 centuries later, just imagine how it shocked his followers in 33 CE. Cognitive dissonance demanded an explanation.

Having made all these skeptical observations about the post-crucifixion appearances of Jesus, let me hasten to add that the nascent Christian movement probably would not have survived without its stories about the Risen Lord. Whether vision, dream, mistaken identity, mystical speculation or actual Christophany, something happened, and it snowballed across that hot, desert landscape both to cool and enflame the distant parts of the Mediterranean basin. Those post-resurrection Jesus sightings refueled the Messianic Hope and breathed new life into the anemic Christian community.

While the reports of Jesus appearing to his followers did the trick in lifting their spirits, these afterlife visits did nothing to clarify the meaning of his life and work. One can almost hear an exasperated Apostle Thomas, the avowed skeptic of the group, say to the Risen Lord: "Look, man, you confused us to the verge of madness while you were alive ... and now you're back?"

He makes a good point. Jesus didn't do what his handlers expected of a good candidate for Messiahship. The Anointed One wasn't supposed to hang out with sinners, traitors, tax collectors, Roman collaborators and other social untouchables. Jesus picked his leadership clique from that sort of rabble. Worst of all, he got himself killed without ushering in the Kingdom of God. "What's that about?" the second-tier of disciples must have asked Peter and the inner circle. The Messiah wasn't supposed to be crucified. That sort of death was an abomination in the eyes of Judaism.

Furthermore, while Jewish apocalyptic prophets had forecast a general resurrection of the dead, nobody had applied it specifically to the Messiah. What's the point? Die, go away, and come back—why not just stay and get the job done?

The primitive Christian community struggled with these questions, not as an abstract duel among academicians but as men and women who had walked with a living, breathing Jesus and now continued, somehow, to experience him after he had died. Second Testament authors rebutted arguments that were already being raised against his literal resurrection from the dead: Matthew mentioned that some people still believed "to this day" the false story of the disciples stealing the corpse. Luke and John reported that the risen Jesus ate with the disciples, proving he was not a ghost but had reappeared with a physically resurrected body. Whatever the actual historicity of these reports, early refutations point to how profoundly the Second Testament community was committed to the historical reality of the resurrection.[14]

While there is no way to establish objectively the reality of these post-resurrection encounters, there is no doubt people subjectively experienced something unexpected, extraordinary and disconcerting after the death of Jesus. Were these encounters dreams or apparitions; were they speculative fancy, successful vision-quests, or examples of wishful thinking? Or did he actually rise bodily from the grave? Despite the recent sensationalism about the discovery of yet another tomb—which some have declared to be the burial vault of Jesus and his wife, Mary of Magdala—there is no concrete evidence that the ossuaries found in the tomb once contained the bones of Rabbi Yeshua and his family. No scholarship yet discovered can answer that question.

I suppose the only way to learn what happened—if you will permit me a flight of science-fiction fantasy—would be to hop in a time machine and go there in person. Of course, given the unlikelihood of time travel and the fact that only a handful of people on the planet speak enough Koine Greek, Latin and Aramaic to actually navigate ancient Jerusalem, this isn't going to happen in the near future.

Even if the actual bones of Jesus were discovered, it would not rule out all theoretical forms of the resurrection, only the type that involved resuscitation of a corpse. Jesus still could have returned in vision, apparition, dream or inspirational thoughts. As previously discussed, significant numbers of people today feel they are in communication with a living Jesus in this 21st-century world. Even a hardened skeptic would have to allow that the testimony by contemporary believers establishes the plausibility of post-crucifixion encounters between Jesus and his followers in antiquity as well as today.

Studies in the phenomenology of religion demonstrate that spiritual experiences with discorporate entities are not exclusive to the ancient world. Modern surveys continue to indicate a large number of people who claim to have had "spiritual experiences" in their lives. Such events cannot be refuted or even discussed objectively, because the very nature of human communication means that once participants attempt to describe a personal experience the reporter ceases to be impartial. My *objective* memories of events are *subjective* recollections for other people, and vice-versa. This is both the strength and weakness of personal encounters with the numinous. Theophanies are self-validating, but only for the recipient. Precisely because it happens within a person, the validity of the vision-experience is above criticism, therefore beyond the scope of empirical inquiry. Just as the symbolic meaning of a dream may be examined and interpreted psychologically, the *content* of any such supernormal contact should reasonably be open to theological analysis.

About the early Christian attitude toward the resurrection, scholars do know this for certain: within a few years, the belief that Jesus of Nazareth rose from the dead was so firmly entrenched that Christians greeted each other with the words "He is risen!" and responded to that salutation with "He is risen, indeed!" Historians also know that from the first generation men and women were willing to die rather than recant their faith in the reality of his Truth. Whatever actually happened—whether the body of Jesus or the courage of his followers was resuscitated—remains the subject of speculation. Believers and skeptics would not be having this discussion 2,000 years later if the early church had not believed Jesus was still available through faith to the individual. To ordinary believers, if not always to theologians, the Christian faith has usually been less a system of doctrines than a relationship between the individual and Jesus Christ. For the primitive Christian community, the crucifixion shattered all the pieces in the Jesus window. It remained for the community to pick up the shards and make sense of the whole.

It was a monumental task.

Imagine yourself a first generation Christian and asking, "What does it all mean?" How would you answer that question? What resources would you employ? In recent times, spin doctors have learned how to ward off negative comments by advancing cheerful interpretations in the face of disastrous events. This is especially apparent during a political campaign. Candidates whose poll numbers are low usually say something like "We're running last in the polls? Don't look at polls, because the only poll that counts is on Election Day. Let's talk about the issues." Of course, if the candidate is number one, the polls will be cited on a daily basis.

People tend to see the world in ways that most favor themselves. There is nothing particularly sinister about this tendency; in fact, those who fail to place their own values and opinions at center stage are likely to be swept aside by every whim and whiffle in the popular culture. The natural corrective to unchecked self-centeredness is critical reflection and dialogue with others, preferably those who do not share a similar worldview. Although this flexibility is one of the hallmarks of postmodern thinking, the ancient world had its version of mental elasticity in the philosophical traditions of Greece. Multisourcing for Truth was a common phenomenon in the intellectual life of the first century, when even great Jewish thinkers like Philo of Alexandria could speak of Plato and Moses with equal enthusiasm. Christianity sprang from this fertile soil. No wonder the new movement was called *the Way* by friend and foe alike.

Powerfully committed to belief in the truth of Jesus' message, his followers took elements of his teachings, life, death and post-resurrection experiences and spun them until the affective merged with the cognitive—until their minds and hearts had processed the Jesus Christ Event and arrived at satisfactory conclusions to the questions being asked by both the Way and its enemies. The natural dynamics of discovering answers to these profound questions from the resources available in the Jewish community and Hellenistic world built the Christian faith. And the greatest missionary-apostle-theologian of them all began his career as the nascent faith's staunchest foe.

The Self-Appointed Apostle Paul

> For I am the least of the apostles, unfit to be
> called an apostle, because I persecuted the
> church of God. But by the grace of God I am what
> I am, and his grace toward me has not been in
> vain. On the contrary, I worked harder than any
> of them—though it was not I, but the grace of
> God that is with me.
>
> —I Corinthians 15:9-10

The first person to leave a written record of his struggle with
the nature and person of Jesus was Saul of Tarsus, the only self-
appointed apostle with biblical credentials. Because he has no
personal history with the Galilean prophet,[1] Paul dwells on the
post-resurrection figure he calls Jesus *Christ*. Paul seems to be the
first follower of Jesus to use that combined-name designation,
often in reverse wording, *Christ Jesus*.[2] For him, Christ Jesus is the
Risen Lord, faith in whom achieves for the believer eternal life in
the Kingdom of God.[3] This is not some eschatological event; the
Kingdom will be established on earth for the first-century church.
Bishop Spong says of this towering figure:

> Paul cannot be taken literally. He did not write
> the Word of God. He wrote the words of Paul, a
> particular, limited, frail human being. But he had
> contact with a powerful experience that changed
> his life, and his changed life was instrumental in

changing millions of other lives throughout the years of Christian history. Can we use his words to get into the power of his experience? Can we participate in that experience and know something of that life-giving power? Can we then translate that power into words that do communicate in our day with assumptions and presuppositions that are in touch with reality as we know it?[4]

Paul definitely has to be decoded for modern thought. For example, he probably believed there would be no more generations after his, because Jesus would soon return through the clouds to judge the wicked and reward the righteous. After separating the sheep and the goats, the righteous sheep would enter God's eternal pasture and the unrighteous goats would be consumed like sacrificial offerings. Yet there is no real doctrine of eternal punishment in the authentic seven letters of Paul. In fact, he is somewhat inconsistent on the ultimate fate of nonbelievers. At times he seems to believe the alternative to eternal life in Christ is extinction; other times Paul sounds very much like a universalist, predicting that everybody will board the Ark before the rains come. He writes in his Letter to the Philippians:

> At the name of Jesus every knee should bend above earth, on earth, and under the earth, and every tongue acknowledge that the Ruler of All is Jesus Christ, to the majestic honor of God, the Father.[5]

Unfortunately, this reckless optimism may be out of character. More frequently he can be heard muttering darkly about the "destruction" that awaits those who will not accept Jesus as Lord. The end fast approaches and decisions must be made. Biblical scholar John Dominic Crossan prefers a seafaring metaphor: "The

Titanic has, as it were, already hit the iceberg, and Paul's mission is to waken the cabins as far and as wide as possible—while God gives time."[6]

Even with this gloomy scenario for the unsaved, Paul allocates no eternal resources to keep the hellfires blazing. Nonbeing swallows up the nonbeliever, a fate that generates its own kind of angst, reflected in this moribund passage that Paul dispatched to the Corinthians:

> For if the dead are not raised, then Christ has not been raised. If Christ has not been raised, your faith is futile and you are still in your sins. Then those also who have died in Christ have perished. If for this life only we have hoped in Christ, we are of all people most to be pitied.[7]

How do the followers of Jesus merit an eternity of paradise while the rest of humanity goes to the trash heap? The answer flows from Paul's solution to the questions the first-century church was asking about Jesus.

Jesus as Dying-Resurrecting Lord

Paul describes himself as a converted Pharisee, but apparently he was also familiar with Hellenistic mystery religions. These widespread and highly popular cults featured themes of a dying and resurrecting savior-god, through faith in whom the individual believer is united with the Lord (Greek, *Kurios*) of the cult and gains unmerited salvation. Because he sees Jesus as both Messiah and Risen Lord, Paul answers the first two questions together: Christ Jesus is the One whom God had raised from death, by faith in whom the believer achieves immortality. How does this salvation mechanism work? Paul asserts, "For I handed on to you as of first importance what I in turn had received: that Christ died for our sins in accordance with the scriptures."[8] To Paul, the death-resurrection events fulfilled scriptural prophecy and provided redemption for humanity, mending the broken relationship between God and humanity.

To further explain the work of Jesus, Paul links the dying-resurrecting Lord of the mystery cult with the sacrificial system employed by all ancient religions to set the balance right between heaven and earth, including the Temple cult of Israel:

> But God proves his love for us in that while we still were sinners Christ died for us. Much more surely then, now that we have been justified by his blood, will we be saved through him from the wrath of God. For if while we were enemies, we were reconciled to God through the death of his Son, much more surely, having been reconciled, will we be saved by his life.[9]

Ostensibly a religion of peace, the prevalence of bloody imagery in Christian lore has caused more than one non-Christian observer to raise an eyebrow. Buddhists are sometimes aghast at the sacrificial demands of a God like the Jews worshipped. Buddhist theologian José Ignacio Cabezón writes:

> The God of the Hebrew Bible is a jealous one that demands the undivided loyalty of its followers, it demands of them blood sacrifice, it is partial and capable of seemingly malevolent actions, to the point of even engaging in violent reprisals against those who refuse to obey its will. Of course, Jesus' appearance in the world is seen by Christians as ushering in a new age, one that reveals a kinder, gentler, more universalistic side to the God of the Hebrew Bible. But the slate of history cannot so easily be wiped clean. Those

> who would identify Jesus with the God of the
> Hebrew Bible make him heir to a divine legacy
> that is, from a Buddhist viewpoint, at the very
> least of questionable worth.[10]

In all fairness to YHWH, there are plenty of instances where the Jewish Scripture shows His painstaking care and steadfast love for humanity. The Psalter is rich with images of God as Reconciler, Rock and Shepherd of Israel. Besides, the Jews hardly invented animal sacrifice, which was practiced in virtually all ancient cultures. Christianity may have raised the ethical bar when it substituted the one-time death of Jesus for the repetitious demise of sacrificial animals; however, one could also argue that in the hands of Christian celebrants the ceremony of heavenly gore rose to a level which the priests of Baal never could have anticipated.

Blood Sacrifice: Common Ground?

> There is power, power, wonder working power
> in the blood of the Lamb; there is power, power,
> wonder working power in the precious blood of
> the Lamb.[11]

In the Academy Award-winning documentary movie *Marjoe*, a 1972 exposé of the fundamentalist tent-meeting circuit, former child evangelist Marjoe Gortner comments that Christian revivalism is steeped in blood imagery. He smiles and advises his film crew to respond to any questions about whether they are saved with the retort: "Yes, brother, and I'm washed in the same blood as you."[12]

The idea of being saved by blood comes right out of temple rituals of the ancient world, where sinners paid for an animal offered by a priest to clear the worshippers' record of blood-guilt.

Not just Israel but most ancient civilizations shared some variation on this theme, i.e., when a person committed certain acts he incurred a debt of sin, which must be paid in blood. It was as though they believed the laws of karma took effect in an immediate and personal way. Trespass and the Divine Justice demanded retribution, blood for sin. The believer could die or offer something else to die in his place, which was far more appealing. Early practices sometimes included infant sacrifice for community sins, but humans wisely decided that goats were more expendable than firstborn sons, so increasingly complex systems of priests offering animal sacrifice for a stipend became big business in the sin-packed world of pharaohs and patriarchs.

This practice was common in Egypt, Babylon, Greece and Rome. In fact, the link between the sacrificial systems of virtually *every* ancient religion and the sacrificial death of Jesus on the cross solved two problems for the early Christian community. First, it explained why God's chosen instrument—Messiah, Prophet, Son of the Divine—had to die. This was not failure, Paul asserts. *This is what Jesus came here to do!*

At this point, it is important to remember that Paul is working out his system at least a decade before the first Gospel was written. None of the people who received his letters had ever read the Gospel of John, where Jesus is promoted from man of Nazareth to Lamb of God who takes away the sin of the world.[13] It is reasonable to think that, had Paul not done his theologizing work, some other construction may have been discovered to explain why the Prophet Jesus died so unexpectedly, but Paul's answer was a perfect fit.

The second function that Paul's original and creative theological interpretation of Jesus' death performed was to find common ground between Judaism and all the pagan systems of antiquity, which had been considered an impossibility by people on both sides. However differently the divinities of Hellenism and the flagrantly intolerant YHWH of Sinai might be viewed by their worshippers, virtually everyone in Judaism and in all the religions and cults understood the necessity for sacrifice in order to set the balance between earth and the divine powers. Paul will argue that by the atoning death of Jesus on the cross, "In Christ God was reconciling the world unto Himself."[14] It was simple, elegant, brilliant. By this device the tentmaker Paul had built a religious community center out of the materials at hand, with doors facing every direction. Luke's Acts of the Apostles picks up this Pauline universalism when reporting Paul's sermon on Mars Hill in Athens, in which the apostle commends the Athenians' attention to an unknown god.

Paul also tapped into the human need to release and let go. In fact, the power of ceremonial release from guilt must not be underestimated by those of us from traditions that view such rituals with suspicion. Even in the 21st century, people hunger for some kind of ritual assurance that all is well again. The Eucharist, Holy Communion, Lord's Super—even the liberal church's equivalent of a sin-offering via the Burning Bowl—all look back to the priest at the altar, raising his knife to slash the throat of a sacrificial animal and grant the worshipper release from the consequences of his sin. However understood, the act of sacrificial elimination of negative self-images and error-beliefs about human worthiness before the Divine has been a vital role for the clergy throughout history, especially in an era before psychotherapy or pastoral counseling.

Priests and priestesses usually became powerful figures in ancient societies for two reasons. Individuals needed the approval of the Divine, and the clergy had the "technology" to free them from a sense of Divine Wrath. There was also an economic basis for clergy power. The priest was permitted to keep some or all of the meat sacrifice as payment for services rendered, by which the clergy grew prosperous as well as influential. The back doors of Roman temples were often the butcher shops where ordinary citizens, Christians included, bought their meat. This is the background against which Paul wrote his famous discourse on eating meat offered to idols in 1 Corinthians, which concludes with Paul's warning that giving the appearance of idol worship might be dangerous enough to make them all consider vegetarianism:

> Therefore, if food is a cause of their falling, I will never eat meat, so that I may not cause one of them to fall.[15]

Paul's Breakthrough: "Christ Jesus Is Lord"

With this background in mind, one can see how Paul's writing developed a model for understanding Jesus and answered several key questions at once. Paul said he knew who Jesus was because of what the man of Nazareth had accomplished, and his death took on meaning only when applied to believers. Thus Paul responded to these questions by function: Jesus—whom he usually called "Christ" or "Christ Jesus"—was the *Christos*, the Anointed One, who gave himself as a blood offering for humanity "according to the scriptures." He was also the *Kurios* or *Lord* after the model of the dying and resurrecting savior-god of the mystery cults; through union with him the believer had access to eternal life. Because of his emphasis on Jesus as the Risen Lord, Paul cast his lot with those who believed that the resurrection was an historical event. In fact, he testifies that he isn't the only one who can establish the historicity of Jesus' post-resurrection appearances. Paul assured the Church at Corinth

> that he was buried, and that he was raised on the third day in accordance with the scriptures, and that he appeared to Cephas, then to the twelve.

> Then he appeared to more than five hundred
> brothers and sisters at one time, most of whom
> are still alive, though some have died. Then he
> appeared to James, then to all the apostles. Last
> of all, as to one untimely born, he appeared also
> to me.[16]

When reading the above, postmodern people are actually looking over Paul's shoulder through a time-and-space window into the first days of the Christian Church. He mentions Peter (whom he usually called by his Aramaic name, *Cephas*), James (presumably the brother of Jesus), and "the twelve," which might be expected. Next, in a breathtaking sweep that expands the witness list off the chart of known disciples, Paul declares: "Then he appeared to more than five hundred brothers and sisters at one time most of whom are still alive, though some have died."[17]

Those words always stir excitement within me when I read them. People who claim to have seen Jesus after the crucifixion still live as he writes! It is as though we are standing beside him as members of the first-century church, listening while Paul dictates to Timothy or Silas. Out that window, hundreds of people "are still alive" who have seen the Risen Lord. We aren't reading speculation about what the first generation of Christians might have said. We're hearing from them in Paul's letter.

This eyewitness testimony was even more important to Paul himself. Paul's emphasis on the Risen Lord required an historical event to be valid, which is reflected in his statement to the church at Corinth: "If Christ has not been raised, your faith is futile."[18] Paul also needed to validate his apostolic credentials, which John Dominic Crossan says was the main reason for including this passage in his epistle to the Corinthians. The converted Pharisee listed all the people who witnessed Jesus' post-resurrection appearances, a recitation that had a secondary effect of

demonstrating his proximity to the original events. By implication, the self-appointed apostle to the gentiles insisted he
belonged in that group, and this association gave credibility to
Paul's claim that his ministry came not from the Jerusalem council of Peter and James but from the punctured hands of the Risen
Lord Himself.

> The thrust of that description is not just its
> emphasis on the risen apparitions of Jesus but its
> insistence that Paul himself is an apostle—that is,
> one especially called and designated by God and
> Jesus to take a leadership role in the early
> church.[19]

Sensitive to the educated skepticism of 21st-century readers,
Crossan agrees that Christianity does not stand or fall on whether
Jesus Christ rose physically from the dead, because his message
did. The good news of the Kingdom revived, and that was the
greatest resurrection of all. Crossan writes:

> My point is not that Paul was wrong but that his
> emphasis on resurrection was but one way of
> expressing early Christian faith and should not
> be taken as normative for all others. [20]

Paul never explored the nature of Jesus comprehensively the
way theologians in following generations did, which one might
even say became an obsession with Christian thought. The apostolic age allowed no time for cool reflection and philosophizing.
Theirs was a hot medium, a rush to publication before the End
Times, more like an Internet blog than an article in a theological
journal. Even so, some scholars have remarked that if Christians
did not have undisputed, extant documents written by Paul,
few researchers of primitive Christianity would postulate that
anyone could have developed such a comprehensive, complex

theological system less than 30 years after the crucifixion. Ideas far less complex have taken centuries to refine in world religious thought.[21] We shall uncover more of this depth as we dig deeper into what Paul thought about Jesus' teachings, his Divine Authority and his relationship to the God of Israel.

What Did Jesus Teach?

Surprisingly, Paul said very little about what Jesus taught. Paul was less concerned with the teachings of a rabbi than he was with the proclamation of a Risen Lord. In fact, Paul decries the importance of both wise teachings and miraculous demonstrations:

> For Jews demand signs and Greeks desire wisdom, but we proclaim Christ crucified, a stumbling block to Jews and foolishness to Gentiles, but to those who are the called, both Jews and Greeks, Christ the power of God and the wisdom of God.[22]

When Paul did mention a teaching of Jesus—such as the rule against divorce—the apostle to the Gentiles felt free to disagree with his Master.

> To the married I give this command—not I but the Lord—that the wife should not separate from her husband (but if she does separate, let her remain unmarried or else be reconciled to her husband), and that the husband should not divorce his wife. To the rest I say—I and not the Lord—that if any believer has a wife who is an unbeliever, and she consents to live with him, he should not divorce her. ... But if the unbelieving partner separates, let it be so; in such a case the

> brother or sister is not bound. It is to peace that
> God has called you.[23]

What this discourse accomplishes, besides confusing almost everybody who reads it, is to give scriptural warrant to decision-making based on one's life experiences. Regardless how lofty is the authority who says otherwise, the Christian will be allowed freedom to decide. Paul certainly yielded to no one in his admiration for Jesus Christ, yet he apparently felt free to reinterpret his Lord. Jesus had taught that there should be no divorce, but in 1 Corinthians Paul equivocates, almost to the point of saying, "Well, now ... let's think about how that applies here." Considering how passionately he believed in his mission, it is obvious that Paul never would have disagreed with Jesus unless the apostle believed that Jesus understood his right to see it differently. Instead of the "God said it, that settles it" bumper sticker, Paul's chariot might have carried another message: "Jesus was a postmodern liberal."

This is an extraordinarily important point, which much of Christian thought has overlooked. For Paul, the specific *teachings* of Jesus are less important than the *principles* on which the Christian faith rests.

Kenosis and the Commonwealth of Holy Typicality

The question of Jesus' authority is an important subject for theological reflection in a pluralistic world. How much authority does Jesus have over the believer? Does a Christian have to accept every recorded saying of Jesus—in the King James language, every jot and tittle, every red letter word—in order to be a follower of Jesus? The problem divides into two questions. First, is Jesus uniquely divine? Second, does the biblical record accurately present his teachings?

If Jesus is the only-begotten incarnation of God, i.e., if Jesus is God in a unique way, the answer to the question, "How much authority?" would be *absolute*. After all, God should know what He's doing. Divine Mind is the only trustworthy guide one could ever encounter, although God has an irritating habit of handing out different guidance to different travelers. Allowing that Jesus Christ is *uniquely* divine—a point I am not prepared to concede—the question of Jesus' authority quickly devolves to questions about what he really said. Even if scholars could agree on a translation of a clean Greek text, the problems of interpretation and application would make any absolute application of those infallible teachings problematic at best, especially when his official biographers didn't always agree on what Jesus said. Paul held that Jesus had all authority under heaven, but he stopped short of equating Jesus with God in a unique and integral way. He comes closest to affirming divinity for Jesus in Philippians:

> Let the same mind be in you that was in Christ Jesus, who, though he was in the form of God, did not regard equality with God as something to be exploited, but emptied himself, taking the form of a slave, being born in human likeness. And being found in human form, he humbled himself and became obedient to the point of death—even death on a cross.[24]

Note that Jesus was in the form of God and emptied himself of his divine nature, because equality with God was something that should not be *exploited* (other translations render it "grasped"). Note also the way the passage begins: "Let the same mind be in you that was in Christ Jesus." How is that possible, if Jesus were in unique relationship with God as one-third of the Trinity?

The "emptying" (Greek, *kenosis*) described here is not a typically Pauline point of view, although the passage is found in an undisputed letter of Paul. Was the apostle hinting at something greater? Did this "emptying" of Jesus prefigure the future of humanity, when we would all have "the same mind ... that was in Christ Jesus"? Probably not. The text allows for a wider interpretation precisely because Paul, writing so early, is unaware of (and therefore unclear about) questions on the relationship between Jesus and God, which later generations will raise. Paul is not uncertain about the authority of Jesus:

> Therefore God also highly exalted him and gave him the name that is above every name, so that at the name of Jesus every knee should bend, in heaven and on earth and under the earth, and every tongue should confess that Jesus Christ is Lord, to the glory of God the Father.[25]

Because of his obedience and faithfulness to God, Jesus has been exalted "above every name" so that everyone "in heaven and on earth and under the earth" should bow before him. Apparently, when Jesus achieved this high status through fidelity to God's will, it became impossible to discern the difference between him and the Father. This is an extraordinary vision of what happens to someone when he/she achieves Christ-consciousness: The perceived spiritual distance between God and the divine individuality within each human becomes nonexistent, and we merge with the Divine Identity, from whence we came in the first place. Is this not essentially what Paul describes?

Paul seemed to believe this union with God happened strictly through the agency of Jesus Christ, i.e., he was following the mystery cult model of salvation through joining in faith with the dying-resurrecting Lord.

> Just as Christ was raised from the dead by the glory of the Father, so we too might walk in newness of life. For if we have been united with him

> in a death like his, we will certainly be united
> with him in a resurrection like his ... So you also
> must consider yourselves dead to sin and alive to
> God in Christ Jesus.[26]

Remove the mythological framework inherited from mystery cults and what remains is another dynamic option. If, in Jesus, there is clear pattern of exaltation through a rise in consciousness to the point where union with the divine becomes a reality, might not this pattern be typical rather than unique to the Jesus Event? Such a viewpoint allows for a commonwealth of holy typicality discussed earlier in this work. If God was in Jesus Christ, reconciling the world unto Himself, does this not also allow that God may be working the same reconciliation in all sentient beings, as they are reconciled to their common divine nature? There is still another possibility, not explicitly found in Paul but compatible with his model of Jesus emptying himself of full union with divinity.

Spiritual Beings/Human Experience

A cliché making the rounds in some churches today proclaims, "We are not human beings having a spiritual experience. We are spiritual beings having a human experience." This observation seems to have originated with the great Jesuit scholar and theologian Fr. Pierre Teilhard de Chardin.[27] However, the full implication of Teilhard's rather profound assertion has not been examined. If we are spiritual beings, how did we get into these bodies? If we are *Imago Dei*, in some wise made in the likeness of God, then perhaps like Jesus we can be best understood as localized outcroppings of divinity itself.

One alterative is to see divine *kenosis* of Jesus as an example of the archetypal pattern, so that all sentient beings have "descended" from full, conscious union with divinity and are themselves incarnations of God-consciousness, albeit unaware of their hidden potential. The purpose for life then becomes creative expression and growth in consciousness until everyone expresses this indwelling divinity. This understanding turns the old formula inside out. Instead of overcoming sinful nature by inviting the Divine to come into the believer from afar, the metaphysical Christian perspective takes seriously the biblical understanding of humanity as "God's offspring" by identifying with the image of God indwelling every sentient. The end result reverses the emptying effect of kenosis by reconciling everyone to their true nature as *Imago Dei*.[28]

Not the Final Word …

Paul was the first to struggle with the Jesus Event and leave a paper trail. The early centuries of the Christian era would see the rise of incredibly complex and sophisticated models of the nature and person of Jesus, of his work and the meaning of his teachings, of his life and sacrificial death. This study in Christology turns next to a crash course in the myriad quarrels over the *nature-and-person* doctrines, which occurred during the formative centuries of the institutional church. Although theologians have often been accused of providing answers to questions nobody is asking anymore, it is nevertheless impossible to comprehend existing problems in interpreting Jesus Christ without first exploring, however briefly, this briar patch of early Christian thought.

As a preparatory exercise before we dive into the brambles, I share the following brief, slightly irreverent poem, written during an evening's meditation on the nature and person of Yeshua Ben Joseph.

Job Description

While sitting alone in an ornate house of worship,
drinking the stained glass and marble statuary,
a little light-headed from the thick incense, and
a little drunk with the sensory input from the
golds and scarlets and purples ...

Just before I arose
to flee this place of excruciating beauty,
Jesus slipped into the pew beside me.

He sighed.
"It's a little embarrassing," the Savior said.

I turned to him, like it was the most
commonplace of all occurrences
to chat with the Second Person in the Trinity.

"You mean, all the celebration
and *praise-your-name* business?"

Jesus nodded. "They call me 'Lord, Lord'
but all I ever wanted in life was to awaken people
to the beauty within them."
He chuckled. "And to snuggle with Mary Magdalene,
but you didn't hear that from me."

"Why not stop the madness?
Call a press conference."

Jesus shook his head.
"They need to believe God loves them,
even if they have to make
a good Jewish boy like me
into a god."

I leaned back,
feeling the hard wood of the pew.
"You can't bail?"

"I have to play the role, Lord and Savior.
It keeps them looking
beyond the daily scramble."
He smiled faintly. "It's a cross I'll have to bear."

"Is there anything I can do? Maybe
write something.
Tell people, you know,
to lighten up on you?"

"They won't believe it.
They think God is out there—in the sky,
in some heavenly dimension.

"They haven't a clue
that all the draped altars,
flickering beeswax and spiced incense
are for them, not me."

I frowned. "Get out of here."

"No, really," Jesus insisted.
"It's all about them finding the Christ within,
like I did."

"You really are a nice God-figure, I have to admit.
Close to perfect."

"Think so?" Jesus smiled.
"You should talk to my mother."

Crash Course in Christological Controversies

(or "How Us Left-Brained Geeks Spent Saturday Nights Before the Invention of Massive Multiplayer Online Video Games")

Computer people sometimes mix metaphors, talking about the evolution of programming as if it were recombination of DNA. Yet the mixed metaphor actually works here, because the historical Jesus has evolved through many stages, but his program retains traces of previous evolutionary steps in all its subsequent iterations. Sometimes evolution takes a wrong turn. One example is the incessant squabbling over the nature and person of Jesus Christ, classically centered around two contradictory viewpoints.

Although Christological controversies have been around since the beginning of the faith, the ancient origins of this ideological battle at first centered around two great cities, Antioch and Alexandria. This chapter looks at several controversies that originated in the differences between the Antiochene and Alexandrian models of Jesus. The degree to which people side with one or the other will shape their whole theology. Before proceeding, a few preliminary remarks about the importance of historical theology are in order.

Hans Küng: Jesus as Decisive

Perhaps some Church fathers felt driven to condemn heretical points of view partly because there were so many wild and interesting variations from which to choose. The early Church was less like a pine forest than a botanical garden filled with a great diversity of species. In this respect, early Christianity resembled its postmodern descendant.

As previously mentioned, Catholic theologian Hans Küng has said that the deciding factor in being a Christian is whether a person sees Jesus Christ as "ultimately decisive."[1] People who look to Jesus of Nazareth as their Way Shower meet all the requirements for a place inside the Christian circle of faith. Küng is so on-target that the present study cannot proceed without considering the implications of his inclusive definition.

Today's religious menu in North America offers an all-you-can-eat buffet, an eclectic array of spiritual fare set forth by self-described Christian groups. Applying Küng's definition—Christians look to Jesus for decisive guidance—these groups all qualify. Actually, this idiosyncratic hodgepodge is nothing new but roughly approximates the great diversity that was present in primitive Christianity. Some Christian groups today are exotic and some are banal; some mainstream and some fundamentalist; others are stolid traditionalist or quirky alternative. In my native country, American Christianity of the 21st century outpictures in forms as dissimilar as the American Baptists and their separated brethren of the Southern Baptist church, who split over slavery before the Civil War and remain divided, even though the muskets and artillery have been silent for more than 150 years.

Contemporary Christianity is bewilderingly diverse: Seventh-Day Adventists and Roman Catholics; Presbyterians and Pentecostal Holiness; Jehovah's Witnesses, Episcopalians, Latter Day Saints, and Eastern Orthodox; plus a host of independent churches and smaller organizations like Divine Science, Religious Science, the Universal Foundation for Better Living, and my own Association of Unity Churches (now Unity Worldwide Ministries). All these share the umbrella of Jesus Christ. Some archconservative groups are quick to disavow any connection between their "true" interpretation of Christianity and the man-made religion practiced by pseudo-Christian cults. If truth be told, one could argue that most of the groups with something interesting to say about Jesus are stigmatized as "cults" by the Religious Right, although the accusers seldom use the word correctly in its sociohistorical connotation.[2]

Even a casual survey of the religious scene shows that people from reasonably compatible cultural backgrounds (predominantly occidental, North American, English-speaking) can look at the biblical presentation of Jesus Christ and come up with radically different religious perspectives. Taking this as a given fact of modern existence, it thus seems terribly presumptuous to pronounce other groups "un-Christian." Any religious tradition that aspires to religious tolerance will require a radically inclusive definition of what it means to be a Christian today, and Hans Küng has provided the definition: Anyone who looks to Jesus Christ as a "decisive" template of what it means to be human and/or divine—as Way Shower or Guide, life-standard or Redeemer, Messiah or archetype, Teacher or Savior, or whatever—stands inside the fence separating Christian and non-Christian religions. A Muslim or Hindu may admire Jesus, but they do not look to him for the best information about what it means to be human and divine; an observant Jew who teaches the philosophy of religion may value the ethical insights of Jesus, but she does not call him *Lord*.

Why Have a Fence?

In postmodern humanity's swelling world consciousness, many will be tempted to tear down all the barriers. After all, isn't there just one religion, the faith of God, taught by an assortment of prophets and saviors throughout history? If God speaks to everyone—sometimes through Jesus, sometimes through Buddha, sometimes through Moses or Muhammad or Bahá'u'lláh or any of a long series of inspired teachers, sages, gurus and redeemers—why must there be a fence at all?

The answer is both disquieting and liberating: *Because there is.* Fences mark where one field ends and another begins. Of course, they are illusory and arbitrary, but also necessary. Homogenizing every tradition into one big ecumenical soup dishonors the fertile diversity of human religious experience. It is certainly true that there is just one religion, but only in the sense that there is only one race, the human race.

The American Civil Rights era revealed that integration does not mean there are no differences between cultures and ethnic groups. African Americans taught their white counterparts that people with a rich ethnic heritage do not simply want to be absorbed by the majority. As an African-American friend exclaimed to me in the 1970s: "Black people—not just dark white people!" Cultural diversity enhances rather than diminishes the quality of life of a community.

The same is true of religious diversity. There are fences between religions, not to keep people out, but to celebrate the boundaries, to describe issues and practices that define all groups. To admire the teachings of great Indian gurus like Paramhansa Yogananda does not require conversion to Hinduism. My friend, the traveling Buddhist monk Bhante Wimala, admires Jesus Christ but feels no need to become a Christian. I've heard Bhante tell American audiences that his goal as a Buddhist is to help Christians become better Christians, Jews better Jews, and Muslims better Muslims. Yet he operates from within the security of the Buddhist worldview. His fence is clearly marked, although there are many gates. That is the secret to diversity without ephemeral syncretism. Not a world without distinctive boundaries, but a colorful and diverse world where the fences have plenty of gates.

Christianity is a chosen worldview. People who consider Muhammad to be the greatest prophet seldom self-designate as Christians, although they accept Jesus as one of the prophets leading up to God's final revelation in Islam. Jews may read and admire the rabbinic arguments of Jesus in the Second Testament, but for Judaism he is not definitive. Hindus, Buddhists, Bahá'í's, Wiccans, Shintoists and New Age practitioners may feel affection for Jesus of Nazareth, but only those who turn to him as the decisive example of what it means to be human and divine can authentically call themselves Christ-*ians*.

The problem of identifying the boundaries of the Christian faith is not found at the world religions' perimeter but along the lines of internal subdivisions. For centuries Christians have argued among themselves about which branch of the faith has fallen off the tree. I believe this is due to a fundamental misconception of the nature of Christianity itself.

Family of Religions

Unless one is willing to attribute self-conscious delusion on the part of people who see things differently, the inescapable conclusion, mentioned before, is that Christianity is not a religion but a family of religions, loosely related to each other in shared symbolism, heritage and sacred literature. Like Hindus, those who practice Christianity have developed a wide variety of options in worship, lifestyle, theology and social ethics.

This diversity is so complete that on social and political issues one may no longer simply speak of a "Christian" point of view, despite the strenuous effort to do so by the religious right in America. A Christian can be a pacifist or jingoist, pro-choice or pro-life, socialist or capitalist, pietistic or revivalistic, Unitarian or

Trinitarian, Universalist or hellfire-and-brimstone, sacramentally grounded or centered in the written word, worshipping in a cathedral or storefront, with modern music, classical music or utter silence. The decisive factor is found in allegiance to Jesus the Christ, however he is understood.

"Culturally Christian, Spiritually Unlimited"

While some might decry this multiplicity as a sign of disunity, the fact is there have always been redheaded stepchildren in the Christian family. One could argue such diversity has been a source of strength, not weakness. New ideas often surface when people interface with others who see the world differently. Obviously, the challenge to any religious faith is to keep its eyes open to new possibilities while remaining faithful to the essential principles that have energized its worldview. This is one reason why I have encouraged churches to consider self-describing as "Culturally Christian, Spiritually Unlimited."

All too frequently we Christians have missed the mark in situations where openness is demanded. It has been easier to condemn the heretic than re-examine one's own beliefs. Christians have not always been willing to hear the dissenter. Too many have suffered for presenting ideas that people needed to consider but which Christian leaders lacked the courage to raise themselves. Thankfully, theology today offers more options, and we no longer impose the death penalty on minority opinions. At least, not officially.

In regard to dissenting opinions, no subject through history has produced more hullabaloo than the endless discussions about the nature and person of Jesus Christ, i.e., the Christological controversies. In some instances the arguments that enflamed the passions of men and women for centuries seem abstract and arcane in the 21st century. However remote from this postmodern age, those original controversies linger today as elements that contribute to the confusion of the modern religious scene. While historical theology is a minefield and must be approached with similar caution, some generalizations can be drawn. Let's begin by considering how to organize critical thinking about the history of Christology.

Two Schools—Two Emphases

In the early years of the Church, views about the nature and person of Jesus Christ broke into two factions that are sometimes called the "schools" of Antioch and Alexandria. The Alexandrian school (based in the great intellectual center at Alexandria, Egypt) tended to emphasize the divinity of Christ, and interpreted that divinity in terms of "the word becoming incarnate." In opposition to this orientation, the Antiochene school (centered at Antioch in Syria) emphasized the humanity of Jesus, and attached special importance to his moral example. Not surprisingly, Alexandria became the center for allegorical/metaphorical (hence metaphysical) interpretations of the Bible, based on principles laid down in Greek philosophy. Antioch followed the traditions of the synagogue and tended to interpret the Scriptures more literally.[3]

These two points of view would clash repeatedly as the Church tried to understand who Jesus was and what he had done.

Radical Opposites: Adoptionism and Modalism

It became apparent during his lifetime that Jesus of Nazareth was extraordinary. People would argue for centuries about what exactly made him exceptional. Was he a specially chosen human or some sort of divine being descended from above? The answer to this question would radically affect theology and practices in the Church. If Jesus was born without any trace of divinity but *chosen* by God to be the Son, then his followers were called *adoptionists*.

Adoptionism: God's Chosen Son

The Bishop of Antioch, Paul of Samosata, taught this doctrine in the third century. The issue was serious. Taken to its extreme, Adoptionism could reduce Jesus' death upon the cross to nothing but an act of martyrdom. According to Church historian Arthur Cushman McGiffert, Paul of Samosata tried to preserve a high theory of the atonement by suggesting that Jesus

> lived wholly at one with God, loving him unalterably and fulfilling his will perfectly in all things. As a consequence he was raised from the dead, was given divine authority, and was appointed to be the judge and saviour of men.[4]

Note that this passage proclaims Jesus *was given divine authority* due to his fidelity to God. Jesus had no more congenital divinity than anyone else. His divinity was assigned to him by God's gracious act; it did not come as a birthright. Paul of Samosata was typically Antiochene in his Christology. Of course, the problem is the Bishop begs the question about how Jesus could exercise "divine authority" without becoming Divine. How did Jesus become Divine, unless divinity was already at least potentially within him? Putting it another way, what would it take to raise the finite to the infinite? Did man become God, or did God become man? One alternative or the other is required to make Bishop Paul's Atonement formula work, but neither seems possible from an adoptionist perspective.

A radical form of Adoptionism, taught by the *Ebionites* (Hebrew, "poor men"), regarded Jesus of Nazareth as an ordinary human being, the biological son of Mary and Joseph. *Ebionitism* was

> … an ascetic sect of Jewish Christians who took their name from the beatitude on "the poor in spirit" (Mt. 5:3; Lk. 4:18; 7:22). In their view Jesus was a human being who lived the Jewish law to perfection because of the descent of the Holy Spirit upon him at his baptism. He was, therefore, the Messiah, the new Moses, who showed the real meaning of the law.[5]

Today several Christian groups hold to the exclusive humanity of Jesus, notably the descendents of 19th-century Unitarian movements in Great Britain and the United States. Although it is fair to say there are many 21st-century Unitarians who describe themselves as non-Christian, perhaps even agnostic or humanistic, historically Unitarians got their name because they rejected the Trinity. Early Unitarians—such as American literary giant Ralph Waldo Emerson, who began his professional life in the Unitarian clergy—held that Jesus was exclusively human, sent from God to teach morality and justice to humanity. This was essentially the Ebionite position. Of course, many non-Christians (e.g., Jews, Muslims, Wiccans and religious humanists) also subscribe to the Ebionite view of Jesus as entirely human, although they would hardly agree that he was the Messiah sent from God to deliver humanity from sin. Nevertheless, the idea that Jesus was totally human is alive, well and widespread.

The Ebionites were also avowed enemies of Pauline Christianity, because they insisted Christians must keep the Jewish law—including kosher eating and circumcision—in order to be a Christian. University of North Carolina scholar Bart Ehrman describes the Ebionites as Christians who wanted to be Jews.

Modalism: Totally, Uniquely Divine

On the other hand, if Jesus were totally divine without the stain of crass humanity—which *Modalists* like Sabellius taught, also in the third century—a totally different view of the cosmos emerges. A wholly divine Jesus renders his life on earth a charade, as McGiffert explained:

> Their original position (Modalists) was very simple and quite without theological complications. Christ is the Father, the creator of heaven and earth. It is the Father that appeared on earth, was born of a virgin, and suffered and died on the cross.[6]

According to Modalism, Jesus' sacrificial act at Calvary could disburse the price of salvation for humanity only because Jesus *was* the Father, paying His own debts. The Modalists reduced feeble humanity to bystanders in this cosmic drama, mere spectators to a transaction within the Godhead. Worse, if there were no humanity in Jesus of Nazareth, then his example was utterly unattainable. In fact, his life was not at all exemplary in the typical sense of a model to be followed. Instead, Jesus had imposed a new, impossibly high standard against which fallible humans would be judged guilty. Only through faith in the Risen Lord could anyone hope to gain unmerited salvation.

Modalism fell prey to the extreme doctrine of *Docetism* (from the Greek *dokeo*, "to seem or appear"), which held that Jesus was like a fully divine actor playing the part of a mortal man. He was not human; he just *seemed* or *appeared* to be. In their defense, Docetists often claimed they were simply honoring Jesus by holding him in the highest place of all, full union with divinity. Whatever degree of devotion these testimonials expressed, they offered no hope that fallen humanity could achieve such an exalted status. According to the Docetist, Jesus is God; humans are not, and never will be. This was a popular point of view among some early Gnostic Christian groups.[7]

When I was in the seminary, one of my professors commented that Docetism preaches much better than Unitarianism. Like the birds that flocked to Jonathan Livingston Seagull, people want to hear that Jesus had extraordinary, superhuman powers, that he was God Incarnate. They are less impressed by thoughts about him going to the bathroom, getting hungry, or, to take a biblical incident, punishing a fig tree because it wasn't the season for figs. Of course, the idea that Jesus could have looked at a woman with lust in his heart is beyond consideration, even though one of his exemplary modern followers, Jimmy Carter, confessed to a lapse into salacious surveillance. Docetism remains powerful today because people want their savior to be almighty and perfect in every way. God came down to us, did it all for us. Humanity has nothing to do but accept the right belief formula, and when we die we'll be magically transformed into angelic beings without making the slightest effort at self-improvement or raising our consciousness.

Although most conservative Christians talk about growing in grace and improving one's character by following Jesus, no actual growth is required for full status in the traditional scheme of salvation. You're either saved or you're damned; there is no gray area. A person who makes a deathbed conversion after having been a scoundrel all his life will achieve the same heavenly reward as the person who has worked lifelong at his faith. This belief is defended along biblical lines, representing salvation as a free gift, not an achievement earned through works. It is presented theologically as God's act of atonement in Jesus Christ for an otherwise lost humanity whose natural destination was hell before faith intervened.

What if Jesus himself had to *work* at becoming aware of his Oneness with the Father? What if he were, in the words of that delightfully blasphemous little tune, "Just a slob like one of us"?[8] Can you feel the cosmos shifting under your feet as you contemplate the difference? Responsibility for spiritual development moves from sacramentally grounded priestly hierarchy to the individual believer. Ritual, however meaningful, no longer offers the "medicine of immortality," and a simple decision to follow Jesus is located at the beginning of the process toward union with God, not the end. In fact, if Jesus truly struggled with his spiritual growth like every human must do, then he did nothing for us at all. Like Jonathan Livingston Seagull, who longed to fly, Jesus did it for himself. Only after achieving his own spiritual growth could he mark the path that everyone must take—a discovered highway to higher consciousness. The author of John's Gospel rhapsodized in these immortal lines:

> "My sheep hear my voice. I know them, and they
> follow me. I give them eternal life, and they will
> never perish. No one will snatch them out of my
> hand. What my Father has given me is greater
> than all else, and no one can snatch it out of the
> Father's hand. The Father and I are one."[9]

Some have heard these words as a declaration of exclusivity: *Only Jesus and the Father are One. Ordinary humans definitely are not, and never can be.* Others have heard John's theological essay via the words of his Jesus as a tribute to the potentiality within every human, a more favorable reading for postmodern Christianity but probably not the meaning intended by the unknown author of the fourth Gospel. Two great movements drew their forces together along this front for the biggest battle of the early church, the *Arian Controversy.*

The Players: Arius and Athanasius

One person whom I regret omitting from the historical profiles in *Friends in High Places* is Arius (c.250—c.336 CE), who was a presbyter (leader) of the church of Alexandria. Although the Alexandrian school held to a high Christology, Arius preached that Jesus was more than man but less than God, which understandably got him in trouble with his ecclesiastical superiors. The problem came from Arius's identification of the *Logos*, or incarnate Word, with Jesus, and then his insistence that the *Logos* was a created being, not the Eternal God. Alister E. McGrath explained the importance of this position to the development of Christian thought in the following way:

> Arius's characteristic emphasis is upon the Son having a beginning. Note the connection between this axiom and Arius's firm insistence upon the unchangeability of God. For Arius, the fact that God cannot change is itself a powerful argument against the incarnation.[10]

McGiffert described Arius' views in language a bit more complexly, yet jam-packed with revealing words:

> The essence of the Son is his own and is identical neither with that of God nor that of man. The Son is first of all creatures and belongs to a higher order of being than any others, whether angels or men. He became incarnate in Jesus Christ, being born of a virgin and taking on human flesh but not a human soul. The soul of Christ was the Logos; only his body was human.[11]

This rather bizarre-sounding formula shelters some interesting ideas, chief of which is that Jesus was *not* God Incarnate, which, needless to say, caused great consternation when delivered by

Arius on the home turf of the Alexandrian school. However highly Arius may have held the Incarnate Logos in his esteem, nothing short of full identification of Jesus as a co-equal member of the Trinity would satisfy his orthodox opponents. On the contrary, Arius believed the Scriptures described a Jesus who started out as a child and increased in wisdom and knowledge as he grew up, which would be impossible if he were God in His fullness. Other ideas that distinguished Arius from orthodox thinkers included the following:

1) The self-subsistence of God; nothing can exist which did not originate with God.

2) God's Fatherhood had a point of origin; before He begat the Son or *Logos*, God was not yet a "Father."

3) There was, consequently, a primordial time when the Son did not exist.

4) God's Ultimate Essence is unknowable by any of His creatures, including the Son.

5) Jesus' status as the Son is not due to his nature but rather to the will of God.[12]

Arius himself had written:

> God was not always a father. There was a time when God was all alone, and was not yet a father; only later did he become a father. The Son did not always exist. Everything created is out of nothing ... so the Logos of God came into existence out of nothing. There was a time when he was not. Before he was brought into being, he did not exist. He also had a beginning to his created existence.[13]

Arius' main opponent was Athanasius (c.296—c.373 CE), who became Bishop of Alexandria in 328. Athanasius' main argument against the Arians centered on two points:

1) Since God alone can save, Jesus cannot be the Savior unless he is also God.

2) God alone must be worshipped, not God's creatures. If Jesus were not God, Christians would be guilty of idolatry, since they worshipped Jesus.[14]

Athanasius was apparently the latest in a relentless line of zealots who brooked no compromise with error. Arius grumbled about the treatment he and others had received from "the Bishop." In a letter to Eusebius, Bishop of Nicomedia, written seven years before Athanasius took the reins at Alexandria, Arius reported:

> Since my father Ammonius is coming to Nicomedia, I thought it right to send you my greetings by him, and at the same time tell you … how desperately the bishop (Athanasius) attacks, persecutes and pursues us, so that he drives us from the city as if we were atheists because we do not agree with him when he publicly preaches: "God always, the Son always; at the same time the Father, at the same time the Son; the Son co-exists with God …." And … all the other bishops of the East, have been condemned for saying that God existed, without beginning, before the Son.[15]

What Difference Does It Make?

Postmodern readers might wonder why the early Church Fathers became so animated over piddling points of doctrine. The answer is because the stakes were incredibly high. Christianity was a young tree; bending its slender limbs this way or that would shape the mighty branches to come. If the universal church had accepted the Arian viewpoint, a much different Christianity would have evolved in the Middle Ages. It almost happened too. Arianism was wildly popular in the fourth and fifth centuries, but key church leaders recognized that Arian success would sooner or later spell the end to orthodoxy.

For example, how can the system of access to heaven through priestly administration of the sacraments be maintained without the fundamental belief that God and Jesus were of the same substance? If God is not especially present in Jesus, how can the priest offer the "real presence" of His Body and Blood in the celebration of the Eucharist? If Arius prevails, the central act of worship during the Mass—Eucharist, the transubstantiation of cup and bread into the actual blood and flesh of Jesus Christ—shrinks from a mystical ingestion of God-stuff to a mere commemorative meal. How, then, can priests continue as gatekeepers to paradise? If Arius prevails, instead of the "medicine of immortality" administered unto the communion of saints for the remission of sin, the Eucharist becomes a light snack with hymns.

The battle was on, and it was fierce, and it was without quarter.

Homoousious vs. Homoiousious (Say What?)

The anti-Arian faction claimed that Jesus had to be "of the *same* substance" (Greek, *homoousious*) as the Father, or he could not act as savior of all humanity's sins. They argued that, if Jesus were not fully divine, he would be limited, finite, part of the problem and therefore incapable of being the solution. Arius and his supporters—and they were legion—insisted that God is indivisible, but God had created Jesus as the Incarnate Logos, a perfect divine-human hybrid, specifically for the task of redeeming fallen humanity. More than human, less than God.

A compromise formula was offered, suggesting the various schools within the Church might be able to agree that God and Jesus were "of *similar* substance" (Greek, *homoiousious)*, but Athanasius would have none of it. To him, the modification made all the difference in the world, which prompted historian Edward Gibbon to say in his *Decline and Fall of the Roman Empire* that never had so much energy been expended over a single vowel.

To solve the problem, the Emperor Constantine called a Council to meet at Nicaea in 325. The goal of the Council was to settle this theological dispute amicably, but in the end there were bad feelings all around and the Emperor waded into the battle against Arius. The final version of the Nicene Creed would be a line-by-line put-down of the Arian position, in which Jesus Christ is declared

> the only Son of God, eternally begotten of the Father, God from God, Light from Light, true God from true God, begotten, not made, one in Being [homoousious] with the Father.[16]

Elitism Prevails

Arius lost in the final act of the drama, because the first Christian Emperor sided with those who said Jesus was uniquely divine. Constantine apparently recognized the value of one faith, one God and one doctrine, all under the mutually legitimizing control of one Emperor. With the attributes of divinity ascribed to Jesus alone, the man of Nazareth soon became judge and ruler of the universe, just as Caesar ruled below. The image of Jesus as ruler was sometimes pictured in medieval art with the ascended lord enthroned on a rainbow, the lily of peace protruding from one ear and a sword of justice from the other.

His remoteness was guaranteed. He was God, and by definition that moved him to a different neighborhood. Soon the Virgin Mary became the intermediary between sinful humanity and the Divine Jesus. Mariolatry elevated his mother almost to his level as the unofficial fourth person of the Trinity. To bridge this newly realized gap between sinful humanity and the Mother of God, Mary's mother, Anna, became the person to whom ordinary folk prayed. They asked Saint Anna to intercede with Mary to intercede with Jesus, who was the same as God the Father. In modern times, many people have hailed Mary for providing virtually the only female presence in an otherwise starkly masculine Christian pantheon. She is still called "Mother of God," but "co-redemptress" has since been added to her titles in Roman Catholic prayer and theology. As a goddess figure, she is fulfilling a spiritual niche that austere Protestantism has yet to address.

More reflection on all these archaic systems of access to God seems in order. Let's suppose a peasant living in the early Middle Ages wanted to "go direct to headquarters," as Charles Fillmore famously said. It is not impossible to imagine the peasant's wife saying, "Pray directly to God? Forget it. God might listen to kings and bishops, but praying directly to the Creator of the Universe isn't for the likes of us."

Going directly to God in the Middle Ages would be like some unknown actor today trying to get an interview with a big Hollywood producer. *Just try it, Buster, and you'll never work in this town again!* Plenty of orthodox churchmen and women would have encouraged the peasant to pray directly to God the Father. When the humble farmer considered the multiple tiers of priestly hierarchy and the corresponding ranks of angels and archangels, it's no wonder he tried to access the system by talking to the Boss' relatives. Whatever happened to the idea that humanity had been created *Imago Dei*, in the image and likeness of God?

One can only speculate about what kind of Christianity might have evolved if Arius had carried the day. Certainly, Christians would have been freed to consider Jesus as an exalted spiritual being, but not exclusively equal to God. There is no guarantee that Arianism would have led directly to an understanding of *Imago Dei* which many people today share, i.e., that God indwells everyone equally, or that logically this would require subsequent beliefs, e.g., the degree to which people express indwelling divinity is a result of their current level of Christ Consciousness. The barrier between Jesus and humanity would have been considerably lowered, enabling humanity to peep over the walls of liturgy and glimpse a fellow creature in the man of Nazareth, someone who was elevated to higher service by higher consciousness. Perhaps the early church might have decided that such a path was possible for all God's children.

It was not to be. Not then. The interactive Jesus would require a few more iterations before direct access was the universal norm.

Toward a Better Model for Today

The goal of this work is to move toward a new Christology, one that is historically linked to the faith that remade Jesus of Nazareth, fully in accord with the One Presence/One Power premise of Practical Christianity, while remaining faithful to the best information available about the historic Jesus. Examining the historical backgrounds of early Christologies has been necessary because some ideas, which descended from early battles, still loiter in the corridors of Christian thought in one form or another. Now our focus changes from history to the present day as Christians look for a Christology that balances head and heart, taking into account the lessons of the past but living in the real world of the 21st century. The search continues for a Jesus that the thinking-feeling person in the new millennium can follow.

- *11* -

Jesus Christ for Today

Love him or hate him, Jesus Christ remains a powerful figure in human consciousness. Even as their theologies diverge on significant questions of doctrine, Christians throughout history have shared a penchant for prayer to Jesus. So many people talk to him that, from a purely psychological standpoint, one must conclude that somehow this unlettered Galilean touches something primordial, deep, elemental and vital in the human mind. Faced with the facts of history, one question demands consideration by students of Christian theology: Why do multitudes seem to need a special relationship with Jesus?

More Than Forgiveness

Some theologians have insisted it is the fear-driven, sin-salvation formula with its centrality of the cross that draws people to Jesus. Bishop Spong writes of the misappropriation of the message of Jesus, laying the blame squarely at the feet of the traditional Church.

> The Church as an external institution clearly craves power and achieves it by keeping its followers in perpetual immaturity. Childlike, uncritical dependency that expresses itself in guilt-laden obedience is the Church's unstated goal. The message of the Christ who, according to the Gospel of John, came that we might have abundant life, is portrayed theologically in our churches as coming to rescue 'wretched sinners'

who are taught that there is no possibility of
doing anything right without God.[1]

Certainly, the Christian faith has no peer among religions in
helping people wash their slates clean and achieve forgiveness.
Christianity is so effective at the forgiveness business that some
churches preach personal salvation to the exclusion of all other
concerns, ignoring the richness of Jesus Christ's message about
everything beyond the narrow scope of absolution for perceived
wrongdoings. This truncated Christianity, often the most vocal
today, has convinced many people that a relationship with the
Christ is only valuable if they feel guilty. Forget about improving
human relations, better mental and physical health, the wholeness enjoyed through improved self-esteem and development of
greater faculties of love, faith and wisdom, true prosperity—
nothing else matters but crossing the finish line to heaven by
affirming the correct belief formula, which absolves the children
of Adam from inherited guilt.

In this gloomy model, the ultimate goal of human life is pure
assensus: You exist to acquire certain theological beliefs, then die
and go to heaven. Could anything be a greater insult to the value
of human life? Listen to Bruce Bawer's withering critique of this
distortion of the Jesus faith:

> Today, legalistic Christians are taught to think
> about heaven in a very different way from that
> which Jesus intended. Many of them carry
> around in their minds an image of heaven that
> draws extensively on the visions described in
> Hal Lindsey's insipid—and disastrously influen-
> tial—1970 book *The Late Great Planet Earth*, which
> presents heaven as a perfect vacation spot in the
> sky, where the saved will not only be eternally
> happy but will also have their appearances

enhanced by the divine equivalent of plastic sur-
gery. (I am not joking.) Legalistic theology of this
sort, far from inviting Christians to enter into an
intellectual and imaginative struggle toward a
genuine vertical experience, demands instead
that they assent blindly to an essentially horizon-
tal set of propositions in order to gain entry to a
heaven that is imagined.[2]

Small wonder more people stay home than attend regular
worship services in the United States today. Is there a motive to
follow Jesus for those who cannot be made to feel guilty or
coaxed to buy fire insurance against the scorching fate that awaits
after death? This chapter considers six reasons a 21st-century person might find a relationship with Jesus Christ worthwhile.
Before proceeding further it is necessary to review the methodology by which this book approaches the primary source materials
for information about Jesus, the Second Testament Gospels.

Which Jesus Speaks?

Contrary to popular misconception, the Bible is not a book; it
is more like a high school literature text, an anthology of essays,
histories, letters, stories, legends, liturgical elements, legal documents, poems, prayers and speculative fiction. Even the Gospels,
which offer the primary source of information about the everyday
life and teachings of Jesus, speak not with one voice but with a
maddening cacophony of countervailing opinions. Perhaps the
most frustrating fact of biblical scholarship is that when you are
hearing the voice of Jesus in Matthew, Mark, Luke and John, you
are really listening to a literary character created by Matthew,
Mark, Luke and John to illustrate the Jesus story. For example,
consider the variations in Jesus' personality at the Garden of

Gethsemane incident just before his arrest, trial and crucifixion. Listen to Mark's version:

> They went to a place called Gethsemane; and he said to his disciples, "Sit here while I pray." He took with him Peter and James and John, and began to be distressed and agitated. And said to them, "I am deeply grieved, even to death; remain here, and keep awake." And going a little farther, he threw himself on the ground and prayed that, if it were possible, the hour might pass from him. He said, "Abba, Father, for you all things are possible; remove this cup from me; yet, not what I want, but what you want."[3]

Mark is considered by many biblical scholars to be the "primitive" Gospel, and his Gethsemane story sounds very human indeed. Mark's Jesus is "distressed and agitated"—who wouldn't be, facing death by crucifixion?—so that "he threw himself on the ground" and cried to his "Abba" for Whom "all things are possible," begging God to let him avoid the cross, "remove this cup from me." The mortal Jesus flickers in this ancient picture, like the black-and-white images of the first motion pictures. Although the long-dead actor is stiff and fuzzy, the reader sees a real, breathing person move across the old picture screen. Mark's Gospel captures grainy images of this historic Jesus, penned and recopied by candle and lamplight. He is afraid, at first unsure, but finally triumphs over his terrors. It is a true dark night of the soul, and most people have been there too.

Matthew's Jesus comes off a little more circumspect:

> Then he said to them, "I am deeply grieved, even to death; remain here, and stay awake with me." And going a little farther, he threw himself on the ground and prayed, "My Father, if it is possible,

let this cup pass from me; yet not what I want but what you want."[4]

Here is a more confident Jesus who doesn't need to remind God that the Father could get him out of this mess. He just says, "If it is possible." Matthew's Jesus also drops the intimate Aramaic term *abba*. Yet the Gospel of Luke goes even further, like a Hollywood remake of Mark's black-and-white original. Luke's Jesus has way more self-control:

> Then he withdrew from them about a stone's throw, knelt down, and prayed, "Father, if you are willing, remove this cup from me; yet, not my will but yours be done." Then an angel from heaven appeared to him and gave him strength. In his anguish he prayed more earnestly, and his sweat became like great drops of blood falling down on the ground.[5]

Note here how Jesus "knelt down" and spoke calmly with his heavenly Father, followed by ministrations of "an angel from heaven" who helped him achieve superhuman strength. So powerful are the Gethsemane prayers in Luke's narrative that Jesus literally sweats "great drops of blood." Mark's Jesus had grappled with events that were spiraling out of control; he was a mortal man who was frankly confused and scared to die. Luke's Jesus has evolved into a self-aware, utterly unflappable Master of all circumstances.

This progression reaches its culmination in the fourth gospel. Of course, neither Mark nor Luke took notes in the Garden of Gethsemane. Many commentators have admitted—sometimes begrudgingly—that no one knows what really happened when Jesus withdrew to pray. The first three Gospels report that Peter, John and James quickly fell asleep, leaving Jesus utterly alone in what was probably the dark night of his soul.

By this image-building, the early church attempted, in the words of Luke, "to set down an orderly account of the events that have been fulfilled among us."[6] Mere recitation of history was never the goal. The Gospels were not news reports but evangelical tracts, messages to instruct the faithful and to attract the wider, target audience among God-fearing gentiles across the Roman Empire. Written in the closing decades of the first century, the Gospel scenes of Jesus in Gethsemane were theological statements based on shared memories and emerging beliefs about who Jesus was and what his brief ministry had accomplished. The deification process was already under way. Jesus the man was becoming Jesus the God-man, on a path to full identification with God as Second Person in the Trinity. John's Gospel, the youngest of the canonical books about Jesus' earthly ministry, denies the whole incident ever happened:

> After Jesus had spoken these words, he went out with his disciples across the Kidron valley to a place where there was a garden, which he and his disciples entered. Now Judas, who betrayed him, also knew the place, because Jesus often met there with his disciples. So Judas brought a detachment of soldiers together with police from the chief priests and the Pharisees, and they came there with lanterns and torches and weapons .... Then Simon Peter, who had a sword, drew it, struck the high priest's slave, and cut off his right ear. The slave's name was Malchus. Jesus said to Peter, "Put your sword back into its sheath. Am I not to drink the cup that the Father has given me?"[7]

After a brief analysis of the text, more questions appear: What really happened? What did all this mean to the early church? It is no surprise that Bible scholar Robert W. Funk says with perfect candor, "I am convinced that the New Testament conceals the real Jesus as frequently as it reveals him."[8] Does this mean there is no historical Jesus available in Scripture? Without some way to weed through each author's eccentricities, the prospect of communion with the Jesus of history seems bleak. Yet failure to find something authentic about the historical Jesus in the Bible would be a disaster for Christianity. How can anyone follow Jesus Christ if there is no biblical evidence of a Jesus to follow?

A Few Solutions

One way to solve the problem is to deny the existence of multiple Jesus portraits and steadfastly maintain that everything in the Bible is historically accurate, which is essentially the position of those who refuse to accept modern biblical scholarship. Go to any "Christian" bookstore at the mall. You'll find volume after volume written with the unspoken assumption that all parts of the Bible speak with the same point of view—*God's*. Besides ignoring a mountain of evidence amassed by the best scholars in the world, this viewpoint flies in the face of common sense. Why would a hodgepodge of authors tell their stories in unison, when onlookers at car wrecks and witnesses to bank robberies almost never agree on the particulars of a common event?

In fact, if all the Jesuses in the Second Testament parroted the same words and behaved in precisely the same manner, any levelheaded scholar would suspect either manuscript tampering by editors or collusion of authors to get their stories straight. However well those books that assume a single Bible voice may sell in a world hungry for certainty, even a casual reading of the Gospels discloses at least four different Jesus portraits, drawn in clashing colors by artists with divergent agendas. If one adds the sketches of Paul and other Second Testament writers, the postmodern Christian probably couldn't pick the "real" Jesus out of a biblical lineup, even if the Nazarene wore a crown of thorns with a halo around his head.

Cafeteria Christianity Revisited

As mentioned earlier in this study, another way to reconcile the need for Jesus-knowledge with the realities of a Scripture written by human hands is to allow inconsistencies to stand and "pick-and-choose" among them, shopping for the best available texts on any given topic. As much as some clergy may decry the cafeteria approach, this is essentially what most ministers, liberal or conservative, actually do. There is nothing particularly heinous about selectivity; it is simply an acknowledgment of what happens when a living, breathing member of a cultural group attempts to interact with a mass of ideas and written materials prepared for another time and place. The problem is not in the picking and choosing; the problem occurs when I select the parts *I like* and declare them identical to ultimate reality while denigrating the parts that *you like* as myth, legend, hyperbole or outright fiction. Or, more benignly, I simply ignore your favorite passages because they don't work for me.

Progressives are content to be literalists on passages such as "Love your enemies and pray for those who persecute you" (Mt. 5:44), but ignore the troublesome words a few verses earlier: "If your right eye causes you to sin, tear it out and throw it away; it is better for you to lose one of your members than for your whole body to be thrown into hell" (Mt. 5:29). Conservatives take passages such as Acts 4:12 literally: "There is salvation in no one else, for there is no other name under heaven given among mortals by which we must be saved." Inconsistently literalistic, they want nothing to do with Jesus' turning water into *wine* in the second chapter of John.

Evangelicals rightly criticize liberal Christians for their selective perception, just as the liberals point to conservative myopia about the contradictions of the Bible. The fight between conservative and liberal Christians often comes down to which parts of Scripture shall be taken literally. Perhaps that is exactly the wrong question. Since one actually takes the whole Bible literally, the struggle for Truth rapidly deteriorates into legalistic brawling about how to read a collection of ancient writings to achieve maximum divine blessing for this or that idea.

Another answer was given by Bishop Spong in a discussion of the fourth Gospel in his book *Rescuing the Bible From Fundamentalism:*

> Literalize John and you will lose this Gospel. For that which is literalized becomes nonsense, while truth that is approaching through sign and symbol becomes the very doorway into God. It is a pity that those who seek to defend biblical truth so often fail to comprehend its message.[9]

Dramatic Contract: "Willing Suspension of Disbelief"

However much I may enjoy playing the Did-Jesus-Say-That? game, the intent of this book is not to itemize phrases or teachings that are authentic, but to look at Jesus Christ as experienced interactively in the life of the church. I assume everything reported in the Bible has intrinsic value, whether it records historical events, illustrates beliefs held by the early Church, or contains spiritual truths that can be understood by allegory and metaphor based on the One Presence/One Power.

Furthermore, the words of Jesus in the Gospels of Matthew, Mark, Luke and John contain within them the early Church's recollections, reflections, hopes and beliefs about Jesus Christ. For all practical purposes, that makes the literary character they created—inconsistent and contradictory as he is—the primary source for the historical Jesus available today. For the sake of conversation, let's assume the whole text of Scripture is a library of human views about life, death, morality, metaphysics and interpersonal relationships. Yet, because the Bible is what it is, one could argue that it must be taken seriously without reshaping its message because the values no longer apply. The Bible cannot be approached as if it were a history textbook; it is a great dramatic presentation of an ancient faith in the words of a people who thought the earth was flat.

Although a particular author may be expressing something I simply cannot affirm (e.g., Ephesians 6:5 says, "Slaves, obey your earthly masters with fear and trembling, in singleness of heart, as you obey Christ"), my discomfort does not issue me a warrant to reinterpret the passage until my cognitive dissonance abates. There are things about the universe I don't like, either. Poisonous snakes and brain hemorrhages are two easy examples. God has nevertheless put me in a cosmos with vipers and aneurisms, and just because I don't like the harm they might cause does not mean they will go away.

Good biblical scholarship demands that I acknowledge the human origin of the text, which does not threaten my faith in the slightest. I am not reading the Bible in order to prove my point of view, rescuing the text whenever necessary to maintain the illusion that Scripture speaks with one voice, i.e., the teachings of my religion.

How, therefore, can I reconcile the clearly mythological, frequently savage events in Scripture with the image of Jesus' forgiving, all-embracing God? I cannot. But because I assume that God is inside all and all is inside God, I am willing to suspend my disbelief and hear the stories, legends, myths, and earlier teachings in their own terms. The author of Joshua thought it was an act of virtue to destroy the cities of pagans that blocked the advance of the Hebrew people into their promised land. Postmodern Christians can no longer affirm that value, but I don't have to assign it to God, just to the author of Joshua. I can also take some comfort in the realization that it probably didn't happen historically. This also frees me to critically evaluate the book of Joshua and compare its values to mass killing in later centuries, a study that must disquiet anyone who knows of the Holocaust and the genocides in Cambodia and Africa.

There are other significant advantages for such an approach. The interpreter's goals become quite different from those who search the biblical library for legal precedents to bolster their point of view. In fact, a postmodern reader probably needs to forget about reading the Scriptures for any kind of authoritative statement and look instead for wisdom, metaphor, archetypes, symbolism and inspirational thoughts—or the lack of these. One can learn from bad examples as well as good ones, as any speaker knows who has cited Adolf Hitler and Mother Theresa in the same sermon. Those who struggle to read the Bible literally or reject it offhand as a warehouse of falsehood share two common denominators: both would benefit from more understanding of human nature and poetry.

To release the power of the Bible does not require 21st-century people to fall backward into a first-century, flat-earth worldview. Biblical interpretation requires an ear for poetry, symbolism, story and parable; it requires reading the Bible for what it actually is— ancient literature produced by people like you and me. Biblical writers were ordinary human beings who struggled to understand their world and live the best lives they could, given the concrete, daily circumstances of their physical and cultural environment. This approach allows both thinking-centered and feeling-centered persons to take the Bible as a whole, even as they would

a Shakespeare play, without the need to make the narrative factu-
ally accurate or historically verifiable. Is the great "To be or not to
be" soliloquy depreciated since there was no historical Hamlet
uttering those immortal words? Was Shakespeare under the bal-
cony taking notes when Romeo called to Juliet?

Dramatists and their audiences enter into an unspoken contract, without which the show does not go on. The actors perform
the playwright's script as if it is happening afresh, right before the
crowd, who pretends to be eavesdropping on the world of the
play. The audience knows these are players performing words
they have memorized and rehearsed. Everyone sitting in the theater realizes they are looking through an invisible "fourth wall"
at scenes enacted for their benefit. To remind oneself constantly
"Oh, this is just a show, it isn't real!" would ruin the experience
for theatergoers. So the proprietors of the theater, the stage crew,
dramatist, director and players all conspire with the audience to
experience a series of events that are not literally happening
before them. Vivid imagination is required, because only so much
realism is possible. After all, it would be a terrible burden to find
a new leading man after every Shakespearean tragedy because
the hero has died on stage.

The dramatic contract between audience and theater company
provides a good model for reading the biblical library. Modern
readers still give the ancient authors their willing suspension of
disbelief, which relieves people today of the burden of finding a
new religion every time they discover some twist in the text that
does not sound true. Seeing the Bible as inspirational literature
sets people free to draw the negative inference, to write their
understanding of life in original Scripture with bold confidence,
as Jesus did two millennia ago:

> You have heard it said in ancient times, but I say
> unto you, Slaves must no longer be obedient,

wives no longer submissive; People must no longer fear dark forces or dread hell's flame. We have grown beyond the myths as history we are now ready to hear them afresh the way they were intended—as good stories.

Treasure in Clay Jars

The Bible is thereby allowed its fragmentation, contradictions, schools of thought, historical inaccuracies, morally repugnant narratives and conflicting images of God. That is the nature of creative material. Not every player in Shakespeare is somebody you'd like to invite to dinner. Taken as a whole, the Bible is allowed to be what it is; people can learn from its ancient lessons and apply whatever teachings and insights speak to the current ethical, cultural and social context.

This is not to say Christians must limit themselves to the Second Testament canon when considering what the word *scripture* means. Recent archaeological discoveries, notably the Gnostic Christian library discovered in 1945 at Nag Hammadi in Upper Egypt, provide a nice counterbalance to the Second Testament and present still a different view of Jesus and his followers and of the diverse and multifaceted church that sprang to life after he died.

In all cases, theological reflection today requires that people be not slavishly bound to the ancient texts or forced to adopt their prescientific worldview. Scripture, canonical or otherwise, can provide a source for engaging in reflection on the Christian message, but written Scripture is not the Christian message in its entirety and never has been. The Unity Quadrilateral of *Scripture*, *Tradition* (what other Christians have said, thought and done), *Experience* (what life has taught us) and *Reflection* (intellectual and intuitive) are equally important and must be allowed their voice in formulating a 21st-century Christology. The ongoing task of theological inquiry is to elucidate the whole Jesus Event and explore its continuing influence over the heart, mind and soul of humanity.

As a committed Christian, I am nevertheless perfectly comfortable with hearing the voice of God through the inconsistent voices of Scripture, because my underlying assumption is that the same Divine Inspiration which worked through the historical Jesus also worked in the minds of the Second Testament authors and guides people to this day. The apostle Paul understood that the message of Jesus had no other hands but ours to do its good work in the world. "But we have this treasure in clay jars," he wrote to the Corinthians, "so that it may be made clear that this extraordinary power belongs to God and does not come from us."

Whenever I read the above passage from Paul, an image of the Dead Sea Scrolls flashes to mind. An incalculable treasure of recorded ideas and images, sealed in clay jars, awaited discovery for nearly 2,000 years. Discovered in 1947, the manuscripts probably represent the surviving texts from a library of the Essene monastic community at nearby Qumran by the Dead Sea. Best guess scholarship holds that the Jewish monks hid their books in a cave during the first Jewish war against the Romans (c. 66-73 CE). Qumran was apparently abandoned in the year 68. If the monks stowed their cache to keep the books safe, they had no idea how safe they were making them.

Since no one returned to claim the valuable work of many hands, one can logically deduce they all perished in the anti-Roman uprising, which also brought down the Jewish Temple, leaving only a Wailing Wall along the vast base of the platform on which the house of God had stood. Clay jars with scrolls in them were not uncommon and served as the equivalent of a bound volume today. They represented the only Bible the ancients knew in the days of Jesus. The Qumran community (if they were the depositors) wrapped their scriptural scrolls in heavy cloth and sealed the jars in pitch. Heavenly treasures in earthen vessels.

Did Paul draw on this imagery when discussing the nature of human life in 2 Corinthians 4:7? Do we hold the treasure of divine Truth within the clay jar of a human body? A study of the text in its historical context provides all sorts of interesting avenues for further insight, albeit not always as fruitfully as the above example.

Informed by the historical-critical tradition of interpretation, shaped by life experiences in the modern world, and guided by intellectual and intuitive reason, an historical-metaphysical method of biblical interpretation perhaps offers the best of all worlds. Through it readers can find symbolic, metaphorical meaning in troublesome, anti-modernist passages that must otherwise be side-stepped by liberals or affirmed against all logic by literalists. I am not required to believe in eternal punishment in order to know that some people create their own hell and refuse to depart from it.

As stated earlier, the guiding light by which this study approaches Christology is that God is the *One Presence and One Power* causing the very cosmos to exist. This foundational belief is expressed in different language by various theologians, but the paradigm of the cosmos is the same. God causes the universe to be, ideates and animates, and expresses as the very power to be. Wherever life, light, love and intelligence are found, God is. The Stucco Buddha offers an illuminating example.

Jesus and the Stucco Buddha

In Thailand, all over Asia, for that matter, there are many statues of the Buddha. One obscure, weather-beaten figure had sat outside the grounds of a *wat*, or temple, for centuries. It was made of stucco and stood about 15 feet high. The eyes were open, with a half-smile on the face. Nobody knew how long this stucco statue had sat there in the courtyard outside the temple. But like the presence of the divine in the midst of life, the Buddha withstood Thailand's political and social changes generation after generation, just as it had weathered countless monsoons.

In modern times, tourists posed beside the sacred image. Sometimes they put their hats on its head or threw an arm around it, as though it was a buddy—dangerous actions that can get the culturally insensitive tourist arrested in some countries. Kids left candy wrappers in its lap. Sometimes people brought flower and fruit offerings. Sometimes people paused to meditate before the image of Gautama Siddhartha, the Enlightened One. The Buddha kept smiling, as though guarding some secret.

The city fathers of Bangkok decided to build a highway right through the courtyard where the Buddha sat. Actually, the government was considerate, offering to provide heavy-lift equipment to move the stucco Buddha indoors. This would be good for the statue, too, because once inside the wat it could be venerated by the monks and photographed by tourists in a more controlled way. After all, even though cheaply constructed, the stucco Buddha was centuries old and deserved some dignity.

One could say that the Christian faith today resembles that stucco Buddha. To become a center of spiritual life again, Christianity has to get moving, to quit lurking in the courtyards of the past. Bishop Spong, whom many Unity people greatly admire, wrote a nice endorsement about my book *Glimpses of Truth*. I had the simple, hand-scribbled note framed and hung in my office. Jack Spong is best known for writing good books that progressive Christians really love: *Rescuing the Bible From Fundamentalism, The Hebrew Lord: A Bishop's Search for the Authentic Jesus*, and his most provocative, *Why Christianity Must Change or Die: A Bishop Speaks to Believers in Exile*. Just as the stucco Buddha had to move with the changing times, so does the

Christian church in general, as Bishop Spong rightly observes in many of his works. Amazing things happen when you take action in faith.

It happened that a group of monks from the monastery decided to relocate the Buddha from outside their temple to a new location. When the crane began to lift the giant idol, the weight was so tremendous that the statue began to crack. Rain began to fall. Concerned about damaging the sacred Buddha, the senior monk decided to lower the statue back to the ground and cover it with a large canvas trap to protect it from the weather.

Later than night the head monk checked on the Buddha by flashlight. As he peered under the canvas he saw a metallic gleam. Mystified, he tapped at the stucco and a piece broke free, revealing more glimmering surface. He called for a chisel and hammer and spent the next few hours carefully breaking the crust off this ancient statue. By morning he was standing face-to-face with a solid gold Buddha—actually, looking up at it, all 5.5 tons of it.

> Historians believe that several hundred years before the head monk's discovery, the Burmese army was about to invade Thailand (called Siam). The Thai (Siamese) monks, realizing that their country would soon be attacked, covered the precious golden Buddha with an outer covering of clay in order to keep their treasure from being looted by the Burmese. Unfortunately it appears that the Burmese slaughtered all the Thai (Siamese) monks and the well kept secret of golden Buddha remained until that fateful day (in 1957).[10]

Today it sits in Wat Trimitr, known as the Temple of the Solid Gold Buddha. The statue, which is probably the most valuable

sacred object in existence and is definitely the largest gold
Buddha in the world, apparently dates to the 15th century. Three
hundred years later, monks encased the image in stucco to prevent its plunder by an invading 18th-century Burmese army.
When Bangkok was built, the statue was moved to the capital city
and left outside a deserted temple.

Could this story from the Far East hide within it the gold of
universal Truth? One cannot but wonder how many people pass
by on the street every day who are, in reality, solid gold Buddhas
in disguise. Is this not the deeper message of the stories about
Jesus Christ? Second Testament authors insist on promoting him
to full, unique godhood, not unlike the claims made about Caesar
and the mythical heroes of Greece. Yet if Jesus was a solid gold
divinity under mortal stucco, what does this portend about
humanity? In the case of the Buddhas of Thailand, this was a one-
time discovery.

What about people? Are human beings merely stucco
Buddhas, through and through, or does this mortal cover hide the
gold of pure divinity, and hide it so well that most people scoff at
the idea of any correspondence between mortal man and immortal Jesus? Some will argue, quite reasonably, for the exclusive
divinity of Jesus, just as there has only been one solid gold
Buddha discovered so far. Yet the great discovery of those monks
in Thailand also means that every plaster Buddha must now be
regarded differently. Who knows which stucco coating might
hide within it an unimaginable treasure of purest gold?

Eric Butterworth picks up this theme in a classic anecdote at
the beginning of his greatest book, *Discover the Power Within You.*
Butterworth extracted new gold from the old Hindu tale about
how Brahma and the lesser deities decide where to hide the divinity of humanity. A mountaintop, sea bottom and other distant
places are proposed but rejected by Brahma, who says humanity

will one day go everywhere. Finally, the Great God says he knows the perfect place:

> "Here is what we will do with man's divinity. We will hide it deep down in man himself, for he will never think to look for it there."[11]

According to legend, that is where they hid mankind's divine nature, deep within each human being, knowing that is the last place people would ever look. With this in mind, let's explore six reasons why a believer today might want a personal relationship with a young man who lived long ago in a cultural galaxy that today seems far, far away.

Six Reasons to Follow Jesus

There are plenty of bad reasons to follow Jesus Christ: guilt, fear of eternal punishment, family or cultural tradition, societal conformity, Sunday church habit or benign ignorance. The enduring power of the Christian message suggests that some people are finding something more than a heavenly fire escape or a place to pay their social dues. As noted earlier, some devout Christians not only follow Jesus, they absolutely adore him, sometimes doing a credible impersonation of stage-door groupies mooning over a rock star. A generation ago when Andrew Lloyd Weber and Tim Rice released the brilliant, revolutionary rock opera *Jesus Christ Superstar,* a massed choir of hecklers from traditional churches castigated their experiment in musical theology as superficial and sacrilegious, but very few critics upbraided Weber and Rice for casting the humble Nazarene as a celebrity. Yet during his lifetime Jesus was no superstar. Struggling to earn the respect of his followers, he failed rather miserably with the people who knew him best—the hometown crowd.

> Then Jesus said to them, "Prophets are not without honor, except in their hometown, and among their own kin, and in their own house." And he could do no deed of power there, except that he laid his hands on a few sick people and cured them. And he was amazed at their unbelief.[1]

Considering the declining church attendance in the mainstream and progressive churches today, an argument could be made that plenty of people who grew up with Jesus have revealed the same lack of excitement as his Galilean neighbors—

culturally related but personally unimpressed. Setting aside the pop icon/rock star qualities in the Jesus promo package, what does a first-century teacher offer that still applies to people struggling to make sense of life in the 21st century? This chapter will suggest six reasons to follow Jesus, though there are many more.

Since the thrust of this project is theological inquiry, I shall explore six lines of religious thought rather than look at mystical, devotional or meditative motivations for following the Nazarene. Certainly there are people who love Jesus so passionately they will follow him no matter where they find him. But this analysis is for people who are cursed with the need to think through their God-given intellect without surrendering control of the feeling nature. It is a hopeless task, since God will always be greater than any system of human thought. However, one could argue that the feeling-intuitive nature is equally incapable of circumscribing God's Omnipotent Omnipresence, therefore application of the sacred intellect is just as appropriate as seeking the divine through the path of the heart.

Every spiritual seeker must decide which path to follow. One could argue that at the deepest levels the thinking-and-feeling natures are one. In my mind's eye, I see Jesus standing in the outer court of the Temple, saying, "Be not afraid of the mind; blessed are those who hunger and thirst after clarity of thought in spiritual matters, for yours is the bumpy road to heaven's side door."

1. Jesus Christ as Focused Divinity. As previously observed, it is beyond the ken of mortal minds to comprehend the Divine mystery fully. One can appreciate, perhaps. Adore, certainly. Full understanding of God's Infinite Love, Light and Power comes much later in the program than life on earth will allow. Other religious traditions agree: Bahá'ís describe God as an Unknowable Essence, and Buddhists flatly refuse to speculate about the nature of God at all. Theologian Paul Tillich said any thought-images of God that humanity constructs must of necessity be affirmed and denied at the same time to avoid idolatry. This reluctance to get specific about God signifies deep wisdom, because human intellect simply doesn't stretch far enough to encompass ultimate concerns.

However great human learning and wisdom can become, humanity will never comprehend the vastness of God. Even the idea that God is a "person" limits the Divine. As long ago as 1932, the great modernist preacher Harry Emerson Fosdick delivered this blistering attack on Christian fundamentalism's insistence that God, Himself, is a person:

> They call God a person, and to hear them do it one would think that our psychological processes could naively be attributed to the Eternal. It is another matter altogether, understanding symbolic language, to call God personal when one means that up the roadway of goodness, truth, and beauty, which outside personal experience have no significance, one must travel toward the truth about the Ultimate—"beyond the comprehension of the human mind." Of course, that is vague; no idea of the Eternal which is not vague can possibly approximate the truth.[2]

The only God large enough to be worthy of worship— the impersonal Father-Mother-Absolute Good—is not only inherently vague but necessarily remote and awesome. That's where Jesus steps into the picture, standing in the Holy Place as a symbol that points to a greater reality. Jesus offers people an abridged Deity. In biblical language, Jesus is called *Immanuel*, or *God-with-us*: Divinity brought into focus by a time-space event in the form of a human life, which flows easily into infinity/eternity by the addition of myth, legend and miracle story. When looking at Jesus, some people catch a glimpse of the Eternal God brought into focus in the man of Nazareth. Marcus J. Borg calls the historical Jesus an epiphany of God:

> As an epiphany of God, Jesus was a "disclosure" or "revelation" of God. He did not reveal God only in his teaching (as if revelation consisted primarily of information), but in his very way of being. The epiphany was Jesus—his "person" as well as his message. As such he was an "image" of God, an "icon" of God, revealing and mediating the divine reality. What he was like therefore discloses what God is like.[3]

The danger, of course, is that the symbol will become the reality that it symbolizes. The map becomes the journey. The road sign becomes the destination. The icon becomes the saint. The idol becomes the divine quality it seeks to represent. For this reason the Hebrew prophets, later joined by Muhammad and his followers, steadfastly forbade any "graven images" of things Divine. You will find no Sistine Chapel in the Judaic or Islamic worlds, because Jews and Muslims find any portrayal of God in art so unspeakably inadequate as to be blasphemous. And they have a point.

Orthodox Christianity has emphasized the divinity of Jesus so exclusively that the real meaning of his life, teachings, death and resurrection have become eclipsed by mythology. Doctrines about imaginary, recompensatory transactions within the persons of the Trinity have shoved the Jesus Event from the crowded marketplace into the priests-only inner courts of the Temple—God the Son pays off God the Father for the sins of humanity by offering Himself as sacrificial victim on the cross. Presumably, God the Spirit is there to certify the payoff. The result is that Jesus is no longer a window into the Divine for most Christians because he has ceased to be human, blocking the Divine-human interaction.

Even when looking to the biblical Jesus for a window into the Unknowable Depths of the Divine, a bothersome question suddenly appears, which intellectual honesty requires. Scholars have long observed that Matthew, Mark, Luke and John present radically different Jesuses based on the same historical figure. This is possible because each person is the unique center of his or her world, and in a sense that means none of us lives in the same universe. Germans call this personalized view of the cosmos *weltanschauung*, i.e., an individual's worldview in general. If everyone's Jesus-figure is powerfully influenced by forces beyond personal control—communal and national histories, preferences among religious beliefs and theological schools, shared culture, inherited language, self-serving political views, issues related to gender and sexuality—where can someone find an unobstructed vantage point from which to view Jesus empirically? Even the first Christians, some of whom knew the historical Jesus personally, enjoyed no such objectivity:

> The Jesus movement very early on exchanged the vision for the visionary. Those first enthusiastic followers were enthralled by the world Jesus encapsulated in parables and aphorisms, but, since they were unable to hold on to the vision embodied in those verbal vehicles, they turned from the story to the storyteller. They didn't know how else to celebrate the revelation. They turned the iconoclast into an icon.[4]

Where Marcus J. Borg celebrates Jesus as "an 'image' of God, an 'icon' of God, revealing and mediating the divine reality," Robert W. Funk implicitly condemns those who "turned the iconoclast (Jesus) into an icon." Both scholars are Fellows of the Jesus

Seminar and share much in common theologically. Yet Borg sounds more comfortable allowing the nature and person of Jesus to carry some of the revelatory burden for humanity. Funk (albeit quoted out of context) suggests he wants to follow Jesus for his *teachings* alone. Borg has suggested Jesus makes a good icon (i.e., image) of God, while Funk wants the iconoclastic Jesus back (*down with all images!*).

The question is not whether you or I shall arrive at the "right" view of Jesus Christ, but rather which view of Jesus Christ is right for you. Traditional interpretations of the Jesus Event invariably arise from one of three basic premises:

(1) Naturalism—Jesus was exclusively human, with no Divine nature. Historic examples include the ancient Ebionites, plus various forms of Adoptionism, anti-Trinitarianism (unitarianism) and humanism.

(2) Supernaturalism—Jesus was exclusively Divine with no human component. For historic examples, see Gnostic Docetism and Modalism, mentioned earlier in this work. Much Christian preaching through the centuries has centered on the divinity of Jesus to the exclusion of his human nature, despite the fact that docetism has been considered heretical since the first century and was officially outlawed by the Council of Chalcedon in 451. Although church councils have frequently rejected ideas that modern Christians might find appealing, the Fathers seem to have gotten this one right. Docetism denies humanity has any connection to Jesus whatsoever.

(3) Dualism—Jesus was both human and divine; examples, Orthodox Christianity, Roman Catholicism, traditional Protestantism. The traditional view holds this bonding of humanity and divinity in Jesus to be absolutely unique; no other being ever had or ever will have *two natures* (human and divine) and *one will*. Because of the "unique divinity" clause, dualism lands

theology in the same fix as supernaturalism. Like Gnostic docetism, orthodox dualism raises Jesus to yet another unattainable peak: He was human *and* divine; you are not. Practical Christianity allows other options, one of which I have taken the liberty of labeling *Incarnational Monism.*

(4) Incarnational Monism—Jesus was both fully human and fully Divine, because there is no other Presence or Power but God. In this last model, every individual human expresses the Divine in whatever capacity available at this level of growth. From Jesus Christ to Adolph Hitler, everyone exercises the gift of free will. The differences appear because people have the power to allow God's Light to shine through them or to block willfully the expression of Absolute Good. The Jesus Event expresses so much Divine light and power and love that looking at Jesus Christ with the eyes of faith, the individual can see as much God as the mind can imagine. Jesus is the focused Divinity.

Following this line of thought a bit further leads to another reason to follow Jesus. The biblical stories and recorded teachings provide an excellent model for communion with God.

2. Jesus Christ as Example of Divine-Human Interaction. If Jesus taught anything, it was that direct commerce between God and humanity was not only feasible but offered the best route to the Divine. He was adamant that God could be worshipped personally, without a mediator.

> But whenever you pray, go into your room and shut the door and pray to your Father who is in secret; and your Father who sees in secret will reward you.[5]

In ancient times a worldwide buildup of practices and prejudices clogged the arteries between Divine Mind and the human heart. Seeking powerful supernatural allies, ancient people often demanded gods who were themselves demanding—cruel, unbending and disinterested in human affairs—and celebrated these hideous saviors through frenzied ritual. Priests representing a myriad of religions and rites, from Israel to India to the land of the Inca, offered sacrifice to armies of gods, and the thirst for cultic ecstasy would not be slaked with anything less than an ocean of blood. Usually animals were sacrificed, but sometimes human blood paid the sin debt for the community.

The modern mind reels when contemplating why anyone would worship deities such as the Aztec gods, some of whom demanded the ripped-out, still-beating hearts of sacrificial victims. Priests who performed these grisly rituals were probably not monsters but ordinary folk who saw themselves with a divine mission in life. The Aztec people believed the sixth and final destruction of the cosmos was approaching, and the only way to forestall it was to offer the Fifth Sun a source of strength:

> The Aztecs believed they could keep the sun strong by nourishing him with a source of vital energy, human blood, preferably the vigorous blood of warriors captured in battle. To the Aztecs, unceasing warfare and human sacrifice were sacred duties upon which the preservation of the universe depended.[6]

To honor petulant gods, we mortals have accomplished superhuman feats. One spectacular example is the Maya of Central America and the Yucatan, who built vast, sophisticated temple-cities in the wet tropics without benefit of metal tools, beasts of burden or the wheel. When lamenting the foolhardiness of the Mesoamerican Indians, the student of religious thought might compare their devotion to other indicators in the Judeo-Christian heritage: Solomon and later Herod the Great drove their people like oxen when building the Jerusalem Temple. This monumental construction project, which would produce the largest temple complex in the ancient world, took decades of backbreaking toil in the hot, Middle Eastern sun. When the task was completed, the descendents of the laborers were never allowed inside the inner gates, because the ground was too holy for their profane feet to tread. Only priests were allowed into the Temple building itself. Even Jesus of Nazareth, as a descendent of Judah and not the priestly tribe of Levi, never set foot inside the actual Temple building but had to be content with holding class and driving the moneychangers from its outer precincts. This sounds disturbingly like the Old South, where African slaves built the mansion homes for their white masters but lived communally in unheated, dirt-floor cabins.

My wife, Carol-Jean, told me a story about a Peruvian friend, whom I'll call Raoul. The boy was raised in a well-to-do, strict Catholic family in South America. His seniors all wanted Raoul to study for the priesthood, so one of their goals was to instill great respect in him for the Church. They spoke with grave severity about the power, authority and peril of things holy. For example, Raoul's grandfather had a Spanish-language Bible in his study, a rare thing in the poor community where they lived. The elders told the lad that this book was God's special document, and that nobody could read it without the blessings of the Church. In fact, because only a priest could understand and explain it, anyone who even *touched* a Bible before he attended catechism classes, made First Confession and received First Communion would be burned up by fire from Heaven.

Raoul was early elementary school age, too young for Catechism classes. Of course, that meant he had never been to Confession nor had he received First Communion. He'd never heard a priest warn anyone about touching the Bible like that, but his elders had said it was so. Still, as a normal boy, Raoul was intensely curious. Why was this Bible so powerful? What secrets did it hold? His curiosity warred with his fears, and finally the recklessness of youth won out. Raoul waited until the house was empty, got a stick from the garden, and sneaked into his grandfather's study.

There it was, on a book stand, bound in funeral black. Three inches of leather-encased death. Glancing at the ceiling, he extended the thin reed in his hand toward the closed book and, expecting flame and smoke to fall from above, tapped the cover. He opened one eye and noted nothing had happened, so he tried again. When his best efforts at stick-prodding the leather bound tome produced no fiery reprisals, Raoul tossed aside the divining rod and grasp the book with his bare hands. Trembling but still alive, he began reading the Bible for the first time.

This attempt to frighten a child into believing that God is a dragon with a bad attitude who lives in the ceiling made Raoul not an obedient priest but an inquisitive teacher, which is probably a better deal for the whole human race. Yet, in all fairness, this kind of scare tactic obviously does not reflect the teachings of the Roman Catholic Church. It was Raoul's superstitious family that tried to keep him away from the Bible. Actually, Catholic biblical scholarship has been quite good, especially since Vatican II. It is, however, an historic fact that both Catholics and Protestants were at one time forbidden to read the Bible privately—it was a punishable offense in Reformation-era England—because the Church felt that lay people required assistance to interpret its complexities.

After the Protestant Reformation, Catholicism was less than enthusiastic about new generations of self-directed Bible readers who might find other reasons to break with the Rome. Reading the Bible for oneself has always been a subversive act. If people can find God through the Scriptures without priest or church, what does that mean for organized religion? You might think the new Protestant churches would be churning out the Bibles en masse, urging people to read and study for themselves. The

Reformers were, if anything, less sanguine about the ability of laypeople to figure out the truth for themselves.

The Reformation leaders reasoned that since they had finally discovered God's truth, nobody needed to think for themselves any more. Although the Anglican Church saw itself as offering alternatives, the range of choices was somewhat limited: you could be Catholic or Anglican. Unfortunately, things got even worse. Puritan England was notoriously intolerant. Until well into the 17th century, there were statutes on the books in Britain that made it a criminal offense to study the Bible at home.[7] The Pilgrims who fled European religious persecution to land famously at Plymouth Rock proceeded in setting up a ghastly reign of terror over anyone who would not subscribe to their rigid interpretations. Quakers were routinely driven out, and when they returned, hanged.

Jesus of Nazareth had a totally different attitude. He seemed to think that God was readily available to everyone, everywhere—no priest-craft required—through Scripture or prayer. Look at the intimate language he used when speaking of God. One expression was *Abba,* usually rendered "Abba Father." According to *Easton's Bible Dictionary:*

> *Abba*—Syriac or Chaldee word is found three times in the New Testament (Mk. 14:36, Rom. 8:15, Gal. 4:6) and in each case is followed by its Greek equivalent, which is translated *"father."* It is a term expressing warm affection and filial confidence. It has no perfect equivalent in our language. It has passed into European languages as an ecclesiastical term, "abbot."[8]

The courage of the translators fails them when confronting this Aramaic term. Marcus J. Borg explains:

In particular, he called God Abba, which is the Aramaic word that a toddler on the babbling edge of speech uses to address his or her father. It is like the English papa. So Jesus called God "Papa"… why would a first-century Jewish person address God as "Papa" when his tradition typically used much more formal terms of address for God? It is a bit shocking, and Jesus may have used this word for that reason, of course. That would be quite in character. But it also seems likely that this intimate term of address for God expressed the intimacy of Jesus' own experience of God.[9]

Even this doesn't go far enough, because English-speaking North American children today seldom used the formal-sounding *Papa* when talking affectionately with their male parent. Another word is preferred, often the first word a child speaks, much to the chagrin of the mother; the best equivalent of the Aramaic word *abba* in American English may be the intimate word *daddy*. Some scholars dispute this, insisting that *Abba* had become a more formalized word by the time of Jesus and had lost much of the kiddie-speak tone of *Daddy*. There is no doubt the word conveys an intimate relationship beyond the formal word *Father*.

God as *Daddy* is a disturbingly intimate picture, appearing once in the four Gospels: Mark's Jesus shouts "Abba!" in terror during his night at Gethsemane, and the cry is so plaintive that no other Gospel author can bear to repeat his childish wail. Believers want a Jesus who is above fear, but Mark's Jesus was better. He conquered it.

If the word-picture drawn by *Abba* is hard for liberal Christians to accept, imagine the impact it must have on folks from conservative traditions. When I was an army chaplain at Fort Leonard Wood, Missouri, I wrote a one-act play for chancel drama called *Gone for the Weekend*. The play is set early in the morning of the first Easter. In the fictionalized dialogue, Mary Magdalene reminds a discouraged Peter, "Jesus trusted God so much He called him Daddy." The woman who played Mary was the rather progressive wife of a Southern Baptist Chaplain. She liked my script but had a hard time with that one line. "I just can't get into calling God 'Daddy,'" she confessed. "It feels too dog-gone personal."

Exactly the point Mark's Jesus was making. God as *Daddy* shatters all pretense to Divine remoteness, bringing God too close for comfort. Whenever church or clergy or Bible or anything else obstructs access to God, one need only remember the intimate relationship between God and the individual addressed by Jesus through the choice of this simple word at the darkest moment of his life. And if you think God as *Daddy* is too intimate, get ready to ratchet up the intensity.

God is neither male nor female, therefore can be legitimately addressed as Father or *Mother*. In fact, whenever humans have contemplated Divinity throughout the ages, the female component has usually exerted powerful influence. Sometimes, the feminine aspect of God has almost eclipsed masculine images, like the widespread veneration of the earth-goddess in pre-Christian religion, or the cult of the Virgin Mary, which has its roots in medieval Roman Catholicism and lingers today. Something in the human psyche knows that God cannot be properly envisaged as an old man with a white beard. There must be feminine attributes in Divinity, too.

Not just Daddy ... God is *Mommy* too. The whole dynamic of the relationship between the Divine and human beings changes radically when this new insight is applied. Could God, as Mommy, send anyone to hell? Would the eternal, loving, all-embracing Mommy ever fail to hear a prayer, or answer one, or provide what is needed?

If you would like to see how powerfully these insights affect God-concepts and self-concepts, try a meditation exercise. Imagine yourself embraced in the arms of God, then change the mode to Daddy and then to Mommy. There is no room for a distant, judgmental Zeus, hurling lightning bolts from his lofty throne, when Jesus' imagery of intimacy takes hold in your consciousness. God cannot be your judge, prosecutor or executioner. Daddy loves you, Mommy nurtures you. Trust God. Trust life. Everything will work out in the end. Jesus provides not only a glimpse into the divine-human relationship; he offers one of the best-tested models of human character available on the planet.

3. Jesus Christ as Template for Human Character. In story and parable, Jesus drew a picture of the highest human virtues. His parables are replete with acts of altruism. The kindly foreigner rescues a mugging victim and gets him medical attention; a father with two sons welcomes his wastrel child back home while bolstering the self-worth of the older son; the keeper of livestock abandons his safe animals to search for one that wandered in harm's way; a spurned dinner host opens his house to the homeless; the property owner shows incredible forbearance with tenants whose actions don't merit clemency.

Of course, I've stacked the deck with sunny examples full of modern-sounding generosity, forgiveness and optimism. One could also look at a few of Jesus' stories and sayings that can be described most charitably as "troublesome": the well-known "Rich Man and Lazarus" parable in which God abandons the wealthy sinner to writhe in eternal hellfire; Jesus' absolute prohibition of divorce; his prediction that most rich people will not turn to God; his rather churlish cursing of the barren fig tree when it wasn't the season for figs. As already observed, the most obvious fact about the Gospel portrait galley is that we have variant "takes" on the character and message of Jesus, as if the Gospel authors hired different actors to play the lead role. "The Good Shepherd," who refused to abandon even one of his wayward sheep (Lk. 15:4-7), simply cannot be reconciled with the teacher who disowned his own family (Mt. 12:46-50; Lk. 14:26), or the merciless judge who told about throwing a sinner "into the outer darkness, where there will be weeping and gnashing of teeth" (Mt. 25:30).

Readers need not agree with the literal sense of the text in order to be honest with what it actually says and gain some benefit from the study. To accurately describe what is happening is not the same as endorsing it. For example, when Jesus curses the fig tree, scholars today see it as a power miracle included by Mark to show Jesus' dominion over nature. The text that immediately follows supports this suspicion:

> In the morning as they passed by, they saw the fig tree withered away to its roots. Then Peter remembered and said to him, "Rabbi, look! The fig tree that you cursed has withered." Jesus answered them, "Have faith in God. Truly I tell you, if you say to this mountain, 'Be taken up and thrown into the sea,' and if you do not doubt in your heart, but believe that what you say will come to pass, it will be done for you. So I tell you, whatever you ask for in prayer, believe that you have received it, and it will be yours."[10]

Context suggests the emphasis should fall on the punch line. One can almost hear Mark saying, "And the moral of the story is, 'whatever you ask for in prayer, believe that you have received it, and it will be yours.'" The parable describes the power of faith, not simply how to respond when disappointed by the misbehavior of trees.

Another powerful illustration comes from the Gospel of John. Although we clergy have wrestled for generations with the ethical dimensions of cursing the fig tree—a question that simply would not have occurred to the Gospel writers—very few preachers have had the audacity to note the profoundly ethical message implicit when John's Jesus flatly refuses to condemn the woman "caught in the very act of committing adultery." Instead he advises her to cease her high-risk behavior (Jn. 8:3-11).

Jesus, in fact, goes far beyond mere dismissal of the charges and addresses this *obiter dictum* to the Pharisees: "You judge by human standards; I judge no one."[11] I have often wondered why those words never appear in the stained glass windows of suburban churches.

When looking for Jesus in Scripture, it is important to let the words say what they were probably intended to say when the authors wrote them for their target audiences, especially if the apparent meaning of the text runs contrary to one's personal beliefs. Clearly, not everything recorded in Scripture reflects the historical Jesus.

For people who are interested in the academic discussion of what the historical Jesus most probably said, the Fellows of the Jesus Seminar have published a series of books in which they discuss the "authentic" words of Jesus in the Gospels. Some scholars of the Jesus Seminar speak of the Gospels as five books, including the newly discovered Gospel of Thomas. Although these men and women are world-class biblical scholars, they are still taking their best shot. No one can say with 100 percent certainty what Jesus did or did not say. It is possible to find useful information about the character of Jesus even in the passages that are probably not historic events (e.g., both the fig tree, because it is out of character, and the words to the alleged adulteress, because the incident doesn't appear in the earliest Second Testament manuscripts). The whole of Christian Scripture points to what the Church thought Jesus was like. Readers can review the assorted portraits and piece together a composite that probably brings us as close as 21st-century humans can get to a glimpse of the man of Nazareth.

The idea that the Bible is literally true and does not internally contradict itself cannot be rationally maintained, and certain biblical doctrines, such as hell, disqualify themselves by virtue of their rank absurdity and moral offensiveness. About hell, for instance, Bishop Spong writes:

> No matter how this question is resolved, the literal authority of the Gospels is compromised. Was belief in hell so common that Jesus simply reflected the values of his time unquestioningly? Hardly, since the Sadducees did not believe in any life after death, either as a reward or punishment. We know only that someone was convinced that Jesus did believe and teach eternal punishment in a fiery hell was an appropriate sentence to pronounce on sinners. Is it? I for one do not believe it. Am I false to Jesus? False to Jesus' interpreters? False to God? I pray not![12]

Obviously, the challenge is to encounter God's Presence and Power in the Second Testament despite its sometimes contradictory accounts. Biblical theology is a challenge because the subject is complex and the subject ancient and somewhat arcane. All those claims of inerrancy and bizarre interpretations flying from pulpits and AM radio stations have not made the task any easier. In Chapter 5 we looked at a simple system for examining any question theologically by applying the four tools of the *Unity Quadrilateral* to the process, allowing *Scripture, Tradition, Experience* and *Reflection* to interact. Even this user-friendly technique requires some background work. The Quadrilateral will be most helpful if people have some basic education in Scripture and

Tradition, can identify the elements of cultural bias in their life experiences, and have logged some time reflecting with both their left and right brains, intellectually and intuitively. The good news is that no theological degree is necessary to read the Sermon on the Mount and learn Jesus believed you are the light of the world, and God really, really does love you.

Once a person has decided how to cull from the biblical impressions a working model of what Jesus reveals about human character, the next step would be to begin applying those principles to circumstances of everyday life, e.g., ethical considerations, relationships and spiritual growth. If his model of human behavior looks remarkably modern, one must realize that the Jesus of Scripture has offered interpretative nuances that Christians through the ages have found applicable to their lives and times. Doubtless our space-faring descendents, while wondering how we could have misunderstood so much, will find in the man of Nazareth a perfect model of what it means to be a sentient creature before the Divine Power and Presence in the cosmos as they venture forth to encounter new civilizations among the stars. This anticipates the next point in our discussion.

4. Jesus Christ as Witness to Human Potentiality. Jesus believed in the common people. He spoke as though potential greatness stirred in every human soul, which was a radical opinion in a world ruled by emperors, kings and nobles. The most benign autocrats were those who used their resources to make life better for the people, but even this generosity had a political motive. Well-fed peasants are less likely to murder their landlords in the night in order to raid the grain stores unmolested.

There are documented cases of slave uprisings that resulted in unspeakable brutality, such as the Nat Turner Revolt in 1831. At first the rebellious bondsmen directed their actions against their former masters, but the slaughter eventually spread to innocent parties, even children and infants. The final act in a failed rebellion is usually punishment of the innocent by the authorities. Indiscriminate reprisals against slaves began shortly after Turner's capture and execution. Hundreds of blacks were put to death, though most were nonparticipating bystanders.

Perhaps the lesson to learn is that violent acts provoke violent responses. No matter how justified the cause—few would argue today that Turner was wrong in opposing slavery—some actions cannot be justified under any circumstances. If the events since 9/11 have taught the world anything, it is that murder in the name of God does nothing other than petrify the opponent in his stratum of hate. The goal of the terrorist is not to educate and convert but to kill and drive reasonable thoughts away.

This unspoken tension between the haves and have-nots has always generated suspicion by one class against another. Property owners rightly feared that thieves might break in and steal their possessions. Theft is still a way of life in Third World countries, where no one would think of leaving a well-furnished house unattended for long. When I lived off the military reservation in an overseas assignment to a developing society, we had a permanent, live-in housemaid who guarded our meager possessions during working hours. This was despite the fact that the house was fenced by a menacing, cinder-block wall crowned with broken glass imbedded in the masonry and topped with coils of barbed wire. I inherited the place from a previous resident soldier, but because of the real-world danger from thieves I never considered denuding the wall of its uninviting accessories.

Imagine an entire world where to be poor makes you suspect of criminal activity. Roman officials hesitated to accept testimony from servants without torturing them first. This was the world in which Jesus lived. How did he handle the barbed wire barriers of his day? He stepped across and embraced slave, free, wealthy, poor, men, women, Jew and Gentile. Christian theology has usually emphasized the generosity of Jesus in embracing fallen humanity, often quoting the apostle Paul: "But God proves his love for us in that while we still were sinners Christ died for us."[13] When read objectively, Paul's oft-quoted observation may not be so much a put-down of humanity as a testimony to the greatness of Jesus and the gracious love of God.

Another possibility exists, seldom considered by Christians. Suppose Jesus embraced slaves, prostitutes, tax collectors, enemy soldiers and blind beggars because he saw them as equals. As Ralph Waldo Emerson told the graduating class of Harvard Divinity School on a warm Sunday evening in July 1838:

> Jesus Christ belonged to the true race of prophets. He saw with open eye the mystery of the soul. Drawn by its severe harmony, ravished with its beauty, he lived in it, and had his being there. Alone in all history, he estimated the greatness of man. One man was true to what is in you and me. He saw that God incarnates himself in man, and evermore goes forth anew to take possession of his world.[14]

What a magnificent tribute to human value! The biblical Jesus associated with people at all levels of his society. He recognized no barriers, because he saw the potential for good in everyone. He knew everyone could reach undreamed of heights. Almost immediately, however, the Church began to disparage the value of being human. Church fathers often spoke of this world as a vale of tears, a mere holding pen that would graduate the chosen few to heavenly reward while the rest of the unsaved herd marched off toward the barbecue pit of hell. Every aspect of human life was suspect, especially those experiences that brought joy, pleasure or intellectual growth.

The argument about human worthiness came to a head in the Pelagian Controversy of the fifth century, after which the Church rejected Pelagius' belief in the basic goodness of humanity and adopted Saint Augustine's gloomy views about human worthlessness. The Church committed itself to preaching that humanity cannot arise from its current state of wretchedness because people are cursed from birth due to original sin. Not everyone agreed, and this controversy has continued through the ages, most recently in the scholarly debates during the middle of the 20th century between Swiss theologians Karl Barth and Emil Brunner.

Of course, Jesus never taught anything remotely like original sin. Return to the words of the Sermon on the Mount for a glimpse of his opinion about human potential:

> You are the light of the world. A city built on a hill cannot be hid. No one after lighting a lamp puts it under the bushel basket, but on the lamp stand, and it gives light to all in the house. In the same way, let your light shine before others, so that they may see your good works and give glory to your Father in heaven.[15]

Nothing in the life and teaching of Jesus can support the idea that people are worthless in the sight of God. We are "the light of the world." That is quite a description to live up to, but to adapt that fundamentalist bumper sticker: *Jesus said that I am the Light of the World. I believe it, and that settles it.*

5. Jesus Christ as Spiritual Master. Healing, prosperity, improved relationships, self-esteem, growth in God-consciousness ... Jesus Christ didn't come to teach theology but rather the art of spiritual living. In many ways, he was similar to an Asian guru demonstrating mastery over the challenges of life. Jesus taught a message of empowerment that helped people lead a better life in the here-and-now. People flocked to him for practical reasons. They brought the sick, and he healed them. They brought their doubts, and he gave them faith. They were poor in spirit and just plain poor, and he taught them that God provides for those who step out in faith. Jesus taught an abundant life message, not just a survival strategy.

A modern example of someone who has believed in the *possibilities* of God is Robert Schuller, who made a career of preaching *Possibility Thinking*. Starting with an empty drive-in theater, he built a worldwide ministry based in one of the most beautiful houses of worship in the USA. Dr. Schuller declared the goal of his Crystal Cathedral was "To help people to believe that they can become the persons God wants them to be."[16] This is, of course, precisely the mystical-metaphysical view of the mission of Jesus Christ, even though Dr. Schuller would hardly have described himself as "metaphysical." Perhaps labels are unnecessary when Truth is One.

6. Jesus Christ as Gateway to Eternity. Finally, Jesus provides people with a gateway to eternity. This does not mean a highway to heaven, but rather a timeless way of looking at life in the here-and-now. Ask yourself how you would look at life if you really believed death does not end consciousness. If life is eternal, what does this mean for human existence? How could people lead selfish, petty lives if they truly believed that eternity awaits them?

Jesus showed that life continues. The undisputable evidence of the early Church is that the disciples continued to experience the presence of Jesus after the crucifixion. Whether he rose bodily from the tomb, or materialized in visions, or haunted their dreams, these post-Easter appearances resuscitated the followers of Jesus and propelled them into the world with a fearless faith that proved too dynamic for the Roman empire to resist. The same energy that rocketed Christianity from the villages of Galilee to all parts of the world is available today. Audacious faith, built on a perspective that looks beyond the silent door of death, can empower people to change the world for the better. Jesus took away the fear of death, so that Paul wrote exultantly:

> Death has been swallowed up in victory. Where, O death, is your victory? Where, O death, is your sting?[17]

The Jesus Event did not end with the Crucifixion, and this historical fact provides evidence that human consciousness will not be lost. The power of such a realization cannot be overstated. When people begin to believe they shall live forever, this hope can make humanity absolutely fearless in the world, and that kind of courage can lead directly to joyful, creative living in the here and now.

Working on Worthiness

A working model for a new understanding of Jesus might include the simple observation that Jesus *was* what we shall one day *become*, i.e., fully aware of his oneness with God, the One Presence and Power in which we live and move and have our being. I have called this concept *Incarnational Monism* because the model is grounded in the belief that Jesus was fully human and fully divine, *because there is no other Presence or Power but God.* Every human expresses the Divine in whatever capacity available at this level of growth. Jesus is worthy to be followed because he knows where he's going, and when people study his life and teachings they can know the destination, too. *Jesus was what we shall one day become.*

Holding this model in mind, let's turn from theory to application, beginning with the universal human need for sense of self-esteem and worthiness before God and in the world.

Jesus Christ and Self-Esteem

> Jesus is the son of God in two ways, [sic] one is
> the same as every other person: we are all chil-
> dren of God, and Jesus was not either the oldest
> son and therefore heir, or the best son, in that
> God gave him something we don't have. Second,
> Jesus was the son of God in a very special way, he
> knew who he was, and acted like it.[1]
>
> —Rev. Donald Jennings

When I was assigned as a U.S. Army Chaplain to Alaska in the
late 1970s, I had the opportunity to become acquainted with the
Rev. Donald Jennings, who was then minister of the Unity
Church of Anchorage. Don was an outstanding minister and
friend, and everyone who knew him mourned his recent passing
almost as much as we celebrated the memory of his good life and
ministry. I dedicated this volume to his memory, hopeful that he
won't have to defend what I've written here to whatever assem-
blage of exalted peers he is currently addressing.

After a year at Fort Richardson in Anchorage, the Army reas-
signed me to a post far north of the Alaska Range, Fort
Wainwright at frigid Fairbanks. I kept in contact with Don, and
when his church decided to bring the Rev. Dr. Norman Vincent
Peale to Alaska, he asked me to coordinate Dr. Peale's visit to
Fairbanks. We arranged a big public meeting for the great minister to millions. My "fee" for the legwork required to make this

event happen was dinner with Don and Carolyn Jennings, and their two special guests, Dr. Peale and his delightful wife Ruth.

During an excellent meal at a restaurant on the Chena River, the conversation drifted to topics far-reaching and exhilarating. I especially remember Dr. Peale's wry sense of humor. "Some of my critics," he said with a wink, "say they find Paul appealing and Peale appalling." I knew this was about his oft-repeated quips, even though Peale's detractors had not meant the remark in the spirit of jest by which he took it. Although he was a world-famous celebrity, Dr. Peale was one of the most gracious persons I've ever met. He listened to my stories and chuckled at all the right places.

Before the evening was over, I wanted to ask him at least one good question, something profound and practical. After all, sitting beside me was one of the best-known Protestant ministers in the 20th century. Like Billy Graham and Jesse Jackson, Rev. Peale was a spiritual advisor to presidents. Formerly a Methodist, he transferred to the Reformed Church—the same denomination as Robert Schuller—in 1932 to become pastor of New York's Marble Collegiate Church, which he was still serving when I met him. He said he always flew home to speak on Sundays, no matter where in the world he was speaking. He was highly successful; over the years his radio and television programs reached millions. Peale's books are still perennial best-sellers, including the mega best-seller *The Power of Positive Thinking* (1952). He was a dynamic 82-year-old when I met him, and he would write more books before he made his transition in 1993 at age 95.

All evening, I tried to find the right question, but nothing came to mind except trivia. Finally, we sat alone backstage before the public meeting. I knew this was my last chance.

"Dr. Peale, I'm fairly new to the clergy," I said. "You're a veteran of many years' service to God. What do you know today that you wish somebody had told you at the beginning of your ministry?"

I thought it was a good question. Dr. Peale must have thought so, too, because he thought about it for a long moment before responding. As best I can recall, here is the gist of what he said: "What I didn't know at first, but learned quickly, is that ministers have to give people something to make them feel good about themselves, their lives and their relationships. If people are hurting, they won't be able to listen to your theology and Bible studies. Help them feel better by giving them positive tools to use in real life, then you can have your Bible studies and such."

What a terrific answer! All through his years of ministry, Norman Vincent Peale had done exactly this: he empowered people to live more effective lives in the here and now through the positive teachings of Jesus Christ. How different this was from the mainline Protestant ministerial education I had received in the mid-1970s. I studied for the ministry at Lancaster Theological Seminary (LTS), a highly respected graduate school operated by the liberal United Church of Christ. The LTS faculty encouraged ministerial students from many denominations to be pastoral counselors and biblical theologians. This approach emerged from a theology of ministry based on Rogerian psychology and historical-critical analysis of the Bible. While there is nothing wrong with a psychological model for pastoral counseling, there is also nothing particularly spiritual about it, either. Clinical psychologists could do it better than ministers, so why solicit help from incompletely trained clergy who are trying to be practitioners of a technique that is basically secular?

CPE Model: Reflective Listening

The answer offered by many Protestant seminaries is *Clinical Pastoral Education*, which provides increased training in counseling techniques based on the psychological method. In fact, my denomination was so convinced of this program's efficacy that I was required to complete a quarter of full-time CPE before I could become an ordained minister.

CPE was a good experience, but I came away feeling that my pastoral education was incomplete. Although this occurred five years before I began seriously studying Practical Christianity, I instinctively knew that there had to be a better way to help people than to say, "Uh-huh. Could you say more about that?" I say this not to denigrate CPE. Clinical Pastoral Education is an excellent training vehicle for driving home the skills of a pastoral counselor. Another possible approach is rarely mentioned in seminary education: Teach your counselees how to turn their problems over to God and expect a positive solution.

Regardless of the psychological state of the people ministers see in counseling, they all have some unfulfilled desire, something that is not happening the way they expected, or they wouldn't show up at the minister's door for help. At the heart of all problems lies dissatisfaction with the circumstances of life, which sometimes leads to dysfunctional behavior. We serve people best when teaching them ways to rise above their discontent.

Buddhist Model: Detachment

Jewish and Christian counselors are not alone in their struggle with worldly problems. Eastern religions have long believed that breaking this cycle of desire and disappointment is the key to moving beyond human suffering. During my ministerial education at Lancaster Theological Seminary, I was privileged to commune with another wise octogenarian, Dr. John Noss, author of *Man's Religions*, which at that time was one of the most widely read college texts on world religions. Dr. Noss was on the faculty of Franklin and Marshall College, a liberal arts college right across the street from Lancaster seminary.

Dr. Noss graduated from F&M in 1916, so when I met him in 1976 he was quite elderly, but he had a wry smile and a gift for humor. He confessed that he had inherited the World Religions chair because nobody else on the faculty wanted to teach the subject. The dean assigned it to him because Dr. Noss had grown up in China, the son of a missionary. He literally taught himself world religions, and in the process became one of the world's foremost authorities on this vast field of human knowledge.

In class, Dr. Noss often read from his own textbook. Why not? It was the best set of notes on world religions available in the 1970s. He also told us many tales that never saw print. I especially remember his account of a Zen proverb about a young Buddhist monk who was seeking enlightenment. The youngster went to his superior and asked for assistance on the spiritual path. The elder monk said, "Did you eat?" When the younger monk said he had finished eating, the elder replied, "Then you'd better wash your bowl." The young monk immediately became enlightened.

Dr. Noss noticed the blank looks on his students' faces—mine included—so he graciously explained that the enlightened Buddhist takes life as it comes. Never expecting anything. Never desiring anything. Not even enlightenment itself. Some Buddhists say, "He who asks is wrong; he who answers is wrong," because to ask a question is to accept the illusion of separation, since all is One.[2]

Buddhists fully understand theologian Reinhold Niebuhr's line about living "one day at a time," which has found its way onto countless bumper stickers after being popularized by Alcoholics Anonymous. The Buddha taught his followers to live for today and solve life's problems by releasing the outcome of all situations. In fact, Buddha wanted people to reach a level of

consciousness where no desire existed. Sounds logical enough—
if we don't want anything, we can't be disappointed when we
don't get it. The ultimate goal of life for the seeker, at least in
Mahayana Buddhism (the discipline practiced by the majority of
Buddhists today), is release from the cycle of birth-death-rebirth
by achieving Buddha consciousness, transcending all desire and
totally releasing the outcome in all circumstances. Dr. Noss
described the Buddhist metaphor of crossing a river by raft or fer-
ryboat to get to the farther shore (Nirvana):

> The nearer bank of the river is this world, known
> to the senses since childhood. From it one cannot
> imagine at all what the Other Shore, far away, is
> like. But the ferry arrives, piloted by the Buddha,
> and when one boards it (i.e., adopts Buddhism)
> and begins the crossing, the receding nearer bank
> gradually loses reality and the far shore begins to
> take shape. At length only the far shore seems
> real, and when one arrives there and leaves
> behind him the river and the ferry, they too lose
> all reality, because one had now gained final
> release in the Great Beyond, which alone is
> utterly real. Thus, the river and both of its banks,
> as well as the ferry, the Buddha, and even the
> human goal which had been all along the ulti-
> mate bourn of Nirvana, are equally and com-
> pletely void. As concepts they had once been the
> useful means of attaining prajna or transcenden-
> tal wisdom, but they are empty now and useless
> forever.[3]

Although the Buddhist goal of total detachment may resonate
well with those who lean toward an ascetic lifestyle, most
Westerners find "lack of desire" to be a symptom of malaise

rather than a worthwhile goal. We are more likely to ask God for help in achieving our desires than to seek ways to stop wanting good things. UFBL Founder Johnnie Colemon writes:

> Remember that you can do nothing of yourself, but through the strength of God within you, anything is possible. Claim your divine inheritance of peace, prosperity, health, and happiness, and persist in making your claim through every thought, word and action. Speak and behave as if you are healthy, happy and wealthy, because you are. Everything you need is waiting for you to call it into expression.[4]

This is hardly the attitude of someone who has no desires. Rather, it is the joyful affirmation that God's desires are good for humanity; anything less than the best is not what God wants people to enjoy. The older I get, the more I find myself concurring with Dr. Colemon. While I have the utmost respect for the noble path and ancient traditions of Buddhism—many of Buddha's ideas are closer to progressive Christianity than fundamentalism ever will be—the fact remains that Nirvana sounds rather chilly and stark to the Western mind.

The Jesus Model: *Thy Will Be Done*

> And going a little farther, he threw himself on the ground and prayed that, if it were possible, the hour might pass from him. He said, "Abba, Father, for you all things are possible; remove this cup from me; yet, not what I want, but what you want."[5]

One could be cynical and remember, as noted in Chapter 4, that nobody heard Jesus pray this lonely prayer. Nobody witnessed the moment when he reach his fateful decision and declared his ultimate faith in God's will regardless of the consequences. The student of Scripture must continually remember the Gospels are really the first-century Church talking to us, that long-ago generation of witnesses and friends of witnesses in whose living memory these events took place. Whether Jesus said these exact words or not is irrelevant; the Church remembered his faith in God's goodness. It knew that Jesus had decided to trust God no matter what happened to him. This level of trust goes beyond petty annoyances to declare that links with God cannot be broken, even in the face of suffering and death. It is a resolute, tenacious, determined, persevering, purposeful, positive, unbendable, stubborn, indomitable, unconquerable, invincible faith.

Despite the jarring medley of Jesus-jingles crooned by the four disharmonious evangelists, one note rings clear as a church bell on a cold winter's morn: Jesus of Nazareth accepted the good and the ungood as if they were the same experience, but he didn't always like it and he wasn't always filled with joy. Certainly, he was not looking forward to Calvary, as the quote from Mark (above) shows. Once he realized crucifixion was the direction intended for his life's trajectory, the next words from his lips were, "Not what I want, but what you want." Something inside him recognized God's love and grace even in the looming shadow of the cross. Although the Scripture shows a Jesus who is not always joyful, the lasting picture is of a person who, after wrestling with his circumstances, released, let go and knew the peace that passes all understanding.

It is faith in God's goodness when all evidence to the contrary presents itself. It is faith in God when life threatens to batter and break a person, and faith in God after being battered and broken. In the magnificent words of the 19th-century Persian prophet, Bahá'u'lláh, who founded the worldwide Bahá'í faith:

> And be thou so steadfast in My love that thy
> heart shall not waiver, even if the swords of the
> enemies rain blows upon thee and all the heav-
> ens and the earth arise against thee. Be thou as a
> flame of fire to My enemies and a river of life
> eternal to My loved ones, and be not of those
> who doubt.[6]

There are elements in every religion that resonate with the faith demonstrated by Jesus. Like the Buddha, the historical-biblical Jesus seems to have taught a Middle Way, a harmonious balance between passion for God and lust for life's goodness. Jesus did not require the Western ascetic's wish for martyrdom in order to test his mettle, or the Eastern guru's detachment from all desires, or the self-actualization model of modern psychological counseling. Authentic Christian faith is far simpler; it is about trusting God in whatever circumstance arises, because Jesus believed that God was a loving parent worthy of trust. Jesus seemed to believe in a gracious universe governed by spiritual principles, powered by God's love and righteousness; therefore, everything will be all right in eternity. Everything will work toward the highest good, even when good results are hidden around the bends in life's highway. Contemplating the cross no longer requires the believer to see the sacrifice of Jesus as blood payment for the sins of humanity; the crucifixion becomes a symbol of ultimate faith in the divine within every sentient being regardless of appearances to the contrary, even death on a cross.

Thy Will Be Done: Activist Religious Faith

Sometimes Jesus of Nazareth accepted life as it approached him, as in Gethsemane. Other times he ran to embrace it, as when he called his disciples. In this regard, his attitude toward daily life was similar to the Buddhist take-what-comes approach, while reserving the right to act decisively, which is a very Western trait. Buddha would not likely have cleansed the temple with a whip or abandoned the flock of 99 in search of one sheep lost in the wilderness.

One difficulty with an activist view of life is that sometimes people make the wrong choice, take the wrong road along the journey. Of course, everyone does this, even enlightened monks. An activist religious faith requires that individuals take responsibility for their choices and manage their own path to "salvation" (i.e., journey to Oneness with God). Here is a potential contradiction in faith and practice. If the watchword "Thy will be done" informs people how to meet everyday life, how do they "let go and let God" without relinquishing responsibility for the choices they make? How much action comes from God's end of the transaction, or does all growth come from human effort? Do people grow because God "reaches down" to us (excuse the anthropomorphic imagery) or because people "reach up" for God? Here are four thoughts about what I have elsewhere called the Asceticism-Activism Paradox.[7]

1. Divine Order Is Not Predestination. It is possible to look at human destiny as a natural flow along the river of life. The most obvious conclusion from this analogy is that the great flood of divine order will eventually carry human consciousness to the Ocean of Oneness with God. Even so, individual choices determine how long the journey will take. People can elect to swim upstream, take side-channels, find short-cuts or jump out of the river and carry their boats awhile. The program of the universe is wide-open, powered by God-energy and permeated by freedom of choice.

Even the river analogy is too limiting. Perhaps life can best be understood not as the irresistible flow of a divine plan but a creative range of human-divine possibilities, an imaginative expression set free with limitless prospects open to all sentient beings.

Doesn't that describe the process of life more accurately? Not a nugatory existence during which people experience an unfolding, predetermined program, but the creation of new programs and directions in continuous expansion. The Divine Artist hands us the brushes and paints and canvas, not to produce a stock image from the God files, but rather to create new worlds of color, texture and shape from the divine creativity within.

When people affirm "Thy will be done," they are not simply accepting divine control of life and its choices; they are opening themselves to choose the good. They are not manipulating God, but rather turning the crank on God's great reservoir within and allowing the creative flow to increase. They are not relinquishing their free will to God's control, but forging a partnership between inexhaustible Omnipotent-Omnipresence and the concrete expression of the Divine Spirit, which stares back from the mirror every morning. Less than this is not adequate; more than this is not required.

2. Destination Guaranteed; Flight Path and ETA Optional. Norman Vincent Peale once told of a flight he took to Hawaii years ago. In those days of lighter airline security, the pilot invited the famous minister into the cockpit and showed him the various instruments and navigational aids that helped them fly from the West Coast to the island paradise. While Dr. Peale was in the cockpit, the captain and co-pilot made a series of slight turns, course corrections. The aviators explained that the aircraft actually flew a zigzag pattern along their flight path. They would drift south then correct north, crisscrossing the direct line of flight as they sailed above the vast Pacific. The captain said they had to adjust the course continuously to correct for winds aloft and other atmospheric and meteorological factors. Technically off course during most of the trip, the plane nevertheless arrived on time in Honolulu.

It seems that Jesus understood the principles of flight 2,000 years ago. He repeatedly urged people to make "course corrections" as they stumbled across the path toward Oneness with God: Zaccheaus, the dishonest tax collector whom Jesus called back to integrity without mentioning taxes or money; the Samaritan woman at the well, whose relationships were a disaster until Jesus encouraged her to take life and faith seriously; Simon Peter, a self-confessed "sinful man," who became the Rock of faith; Mary and Martha, two sisters who represented reflective and active faith; the "rich young ruler" whose inability to handle wealth had become a burden that he could neither bear nor release; the woman caught in the act of adultery, whom Jesus challenged to make better choices; and the list goes on and on.

The Second Testament shows a wild explosion of personal growth among the followers of Jesus. These transformations are even more amazing when one considers that the ancient world believed a person's character was fixed and could not change. Jesus called people to begin a journey, and his disciples stumbled across the flight trajectory to higher consciousness as they followed their best route along the path demonstrated by their Way Shower.

3. God Does Not Compel Us to Grow. Nobody will force you to stop beating your head on the wall. Alcoholics and other compulsives know what it means to say, "I had to hit bottom before taking responsibility for my life." At first, they blame parents, siblings, inadequate schools, poverty, the injustice of society, or just bad luck. Sooner or later, compulsives seeking genuine recovery are forced to admit that the source of their difficulties is the person they have made themselves. Poor choices continue to cause problems, and change occurs only when people take responsibility for their lives.

When I was a military chaplain I frequently dealt with soldiers' family problems, often working with the spouses of military members. I've counseled both dependent wives and dependent husbands, but one incident has stayed in mind, even though it happened in the late 1970s. I was the on-call duty chaplain at Fort Leonard Wood, Missouri, when I received a request to go to a soldier's home in the housing area and give his wife, whom I'll call Gretchen, a ride to the bus station.

Gretchen told me en route that she was leaving her husband. He had beaten her up, again, but she was leaving for good. She was a pleasant, soft-spoken woman with an accent that suggested a childhood in the Southern Appalachians. During the short ride, Gretchen also let slip that this was her fourth marriage.

"Did any of the others hit you?" I asked.

"They all did," she confessed.

Experienced clergy know that pastors earn the right to intervene in someone's problems by building long-term relationships with members of their parish. However, I knew I'd never see Gretchen again, and Divine Order had placed her in my car this night and given me the opportunity to say something she might never hear again. So I took the risk.

"Gretchen, do you think there might be a reason you've chosen four battering husbands in a row?"

She nodded slowly. "Maybe bad luck."

I shook my head. "Sorry, I don't believe in luck."

"I always thought, *If I'm good enough, he won't hit me.* I tried hard to be good, but he hit me anyway. What am I doing wrong?"

The seminary-trained pastoral counselor inside me wanted to scream, *Nothing, it's the battering jackass you married who's wrong!* After all, he had punched, kicked and spat on her, and no woman deserves that. No man, woman or child should be beaten. *It is wrong, wrong, wrong.*

The Christian minister inside me knew that people tend to attract experiences to themselves by consciousness, and that heaping verbal abuse on the battering spouse was no help to the victim of abuse. Gretchen was my concern, even for the brief ride we shared to the bus station that night. She had been choosing to remain in a system of abuse, but now she wanted the hurting to stop.

"Forgive me for being so direct, but I'll probably never see you again, and I need you to hear something. You're attracting abusive men like you're wearing a 'hit me' magnet. There must be something going on here—something in the personality profile of a battering husband that you find appealing. If you don't find out why you're making this mistake, you're very likely going to do it again."

She wiped a tear. "What should I do?"

"Find a good counselor who will work with you to identify the reasons for your self-defeating choices. Start working on yourself by affirming, again and again: *I am the precious child of God, I deserve to be happy, to be loved, to be safe, and to be cherished in all my relationships.* Repeat this little prayer, three times, whenever you think anything unkind about yourself, or any time you feel worried about the future. Will you do that?"

She said she would, and asked me to write down the affirmation. I did, adding the toll-free number for the Silent Unity prayer line at the bottom of the paper.[8] She asked for prayer, which I offered at the bus station, then she boarded a Greyhound for somewhere in the Deep South. I have no idea what happened to her, but remaining faithful to the faith taught by Jesus Christ required me to speak up and offer her an alternative view of herself. She was more than anyone had ever told her she could be— *the precious child of God.*

God does not compel self-improvement any more than gravity compels upright walking. Nevertheless, there is more than a little reason for hope, as the final point will demonstrate.

4. Everybody Will Get It Right Eventually, So Relax and Be Kind. There is a serious misunderstanding that has often caused some people to take a more hands-off role in church growth and outreach. Psalm 103 proclaims: "The Lord has established his throne in the heavens, and his kingdom rules over all." The contemporary expression of this sentiment is found the oft-repeated truism *"God has everything under control."* According to this view, all one has to do is *"Let go and let God"* work the perfect outcome to any circumstance. Why, then, should a church be so impatient as to organize an outreach committee or send members to locate kindred souls in the community? Doubtless, other people comfort themselves by remembering, rightly, that everybody will eventually come to Christ-consciousness. Shall this smug self-confidence allow spiritually progressive people to evade the responsibility of sharing their understanding of the faith simply because they recognize the ultimate conclusion of human spiritual growth?

Plato said, "Be kind, for everyone you meet is fighting a hard battle."[9] As a young man, I would repeat those words when confronted by someone who vexed me. Typical of a young person growing up in the 1960s, I had a good working knowledge of how everything should be done and how everyone should behave. As I grew older, I became a little less certain about my status as a sociopolitical arbiter. I also found it necessary to modify slightly the bromides I'd been contemplating. To render it compliant with the principles of progressive Christianity, I revised Plato's maxim: "Be kind, for everyone you meet is working at their own pace. They'll get it, eventually." I have found this idea can be quite liberating for some people, especially those who come from a church tradition that heavily emphasizes its mission to save a heathen world.

If you drive around the town where you live any Sunday morning, you'll probably note church signboards that announce sermons about converting your community to Christianity. Although many of my fellow religious progressives sneer at evangelism, the Christian faith began as a missionary movement within Judaism, and to this day it has continued to spread by a combination of institutional outreach and word of mouth. Presenting the teachings of Jesus Christ to unchurched people—those who have no religious preference or those who are nominally members of a religion but dissatisfied with their faith—does not have to be an act of hostility or cultural imperialism.

Studies show that most church members would not be there if someone had not told them about this exciting gathering of the Christian family. In this respect, we are not alone. Other studies have shown that more than 75 percent of the people who join a church in North America do so because they were invited by a friend or relative. In fact, the fastest growing churches are those that take outreach seriously and inspire enthusiasm in their congregations to reach out to the unchurched of their communities.

5. Don't Hide Your Light Under a Basket. In some progressive Christian circles, it often feels like growth in a local church happens despite the current membership's best efforts to sabotage church expansion. Anecdotal evidence suggests that fast-growing churches are built around a combination of dynamic ministers, inspirational worship events, and rockin' spiritual music programs. Until lately, there has been little concerted effort to plan comprehensively for intentional growth among some progressive denominations. They are catching up fast, and their leaders are wisely seeking advice from friends in strange places.

For example, I attended a workshop at Dr. Rick Warren's Saddleback Baptist Church in Orange County, California. I looked across the vast sea of tables at *thousands* of pastors, who had come from virtually every Christian denomination, all gathered in a gymnasium-style convention hall to hear Pastor Rick trumpet the need for transformational preaching and intentional growth. I must confess, before attending this conference, I often drove past the big fundamentalist churches in town, smirking self-righteously about how the evangelical clergy were deceiving people and feeding on fears of hellfire. Although I still believe God is totally incapable of punishing anybody for anything—life's missed opportunities punish us enough, when self-defeating options are imprudently embraced—I learned from sharing donuts and coffee with "fundamentalist" clergy that they are often meeting the needs of their congregations in a fundamental way.

As Norman Vincent Peale had advised me, many evangelical ministers are well aware that people need to be affirmed, feel good about themselves, believe there is reason for hope, and be given tools to climb life's mountains. They know people also want to believe they are part of something grand and glorious, and they can make a difference in the world. That sense of God's presence and power is what the most successful conservative churches are providing, and people are eating it up. There is so much emptiness in the contemporary world that *any* message which offers people meaning, purpose, self-improvement and reconciliation will pour hope into the values-vacuum of this culture of postmodern nonbelievers. People who are desperate for a return to religious significance in their lives often find this kind of enthusiasm persuasive, compelling, irresistible.

Is there anything in the preceding message that could not be proclaimed by any progressive Christian church? In fact, one could argue that progressive Christianity has the ultimate self-empowerment agenda, better reconciliation techniques, and the most powerful message available to infuse a sense of the holy in everyday life.

What we progressives have been lacking is zeal, which is one of Charles Fillmore's *Twelve Powers of Man*. Perhaps the time has come to take a lesson from conservative Christian brothers and sisters about becoming intentional proclaimers of the Good News. After all, haven't people heard the bad news long enough? Imagine what would happen if an excited, well-trained, well-organized congregation of progressive Christians decided to acquaint every unchurched soul in their community with the opportunities for growth and wholeness available through Christ-centered teachings and techniques available today? Churches would need to build new sanctuaries to hold the over-flow crowds! Of course, even while planning intentional growth, some progressive congregations will see each person as the precious child of God, each deserving an opportunity to realize his or her great potential. This right to self-esteem was guaranteed by Jesus Christ when he proclaimed the magnificent qualities of his fellow humans: You are the light of the world. A city built on a hill cannot be hid. No one after lighting a lamp puts it under the bushel basket, but on the lamp stand, and it gives light to all in the house. In the same way, let your light shine before others, so that they may see your good works and give glory to your Father in heaven.[10]

Courage for Living

One cold, moonlit evening in the early days of the American republic, a traveler reached the Mississippi River on foot. The river was covered in a sheet of ice topped with snow, but the traveler had no way of knowing whether the ice would support his weight. Night was falling and he was still quite far from the nearest settlement, so he inched out onto the snowy surface. Creeping on his hands and knees to distribute his weight, he timidly made his way toward the far bank. When he was halfway across he heard the sound of lusty singing behind him. James S. Hewett describes what happened next:

> Out of the dusk there came a man, driving a horse-drawn load of coal across the ice and singing merrily as he went his way. Here he was—on his hands and knees, trembling lest the ice be not strong enough to bear him up! And there, as if whisked away by the winter's wind, went the man, his horses, his sleigh, and his load of coal, upheld by the same ice on which he was creeping![11]

The coal wagon teamster had something far better than a road map; he had life experience. He had already crossed that frozen river and knew it would bear him up. People who follow Jesus the Christ have told me they enjoy the same kind of certainty about life's dangers and challenges. They have decided that Jesus is the key to safe passage through the winters and summers of human life. His message of agape, selfless love based on an unshakeable trust in God, can transform trembling fear into ebullient confidence.

- 14 -

Jesus Christ and Relationships:
The Four Kinds of Love

This is my commandment, that you love one
another as I have loved you.[1]

We have no way of knowing whether these immortal words
were spoken by Jesus or imported from the imagination of the
unknown author of the Gospel of John. However, John's telling of
the *good news* makes it clear that at least some members of the
first-century Christian community believed Jesus had taught a
gospel of love. There are many possible ways to arrange the
themes found in the record of what early Christians said Jesus
said. One could arguably contend that the main emphasis of
Jesus' proclamation was an admonition to remain faithful to the
ethical demands of Judaism while awaiting the imminent advent
of divine justice in the coming kingdom of God. Other possible
lenses through which his recorded words could be interpreted
include ways of earning personal salvation through acts of faith
and works, or achieving mystical union with God through faith
in Jesus himself.

However, throughout the history of biblical interpretation the
theme of Jesus as the embodiment of divine love has found special favor among contemplatives, mystics and humanitarians.
Small wonder. Love is not controversial, offering interpreters the
dual advantages of warmth and ambiguity. In fact, love is probably the most written about and least understood of all human

experiences, and because few serious thinkers have ever attacked the idea of love as a human virtue and divine quality, basing one's Christology on love seems to steer a safe course through the dangerous waters of biblical hermeneutics.

Yet, despite the ongoing obsession of Western civilization with love, humanity needs to face the fact that its Information Age culture knows very little about this most powerful motivator in daily life. This is true even though Western society is inundated with love-talk. Consider that most North Americans know more about professional sports than they do about love, even though some theologians believe love is the very force that holds the cosmos together.

The Bible, of course, brims with love-talk: *God so loved the world ... the disciple whom Jesus loved ... love bears all things ... who can separate us from the love of God?* And not just in the Second Testament. My unscientific quick check of a modern English translation counted over 120 references to "love" in the Book of Psalms alone. Beyond the Bible, world literature is flush with words of love. Even though Shakespeare's heroines were played by prepubescent boys in stodgy Elizabethan England, the Bard still managed to splash love across the pages of his scripts like a drunken sailor spilling wine. I suspect most people have given little thought to whether Shakespeare's sonnets were written for boyfriends or girlfriends; beautiful words of love work for all flavors.

Much of the popular music written in the 20th and 21st centuries has been about love. I would hazard a guess that most people are hard pressed to name a few popular tunes that are NOT love songs. A generation ago the Beatles proclaimed, "All you need is love." *Ra-ta-ta-ta-ta.* Love was all they needed to make millions. With their careers established, the Beatles branched out into pure storytelling ballads like "Eleanor Rigby" and creative excursions like the *Sgt. Pepper, Magical Mystery Tour,* and *Abbey Road* albums. Beatlemania began with "I Wanna Hold Your

Hand" and "She Loves You," and The Fab Four continued to produce quality love music until they disbanded. One of their last, best offerings before the group broke up was "The Long and Winding Road," a hauntingly beautiful love song.

Movies must have a love interest to maximize their appeal at the box office. Sometimes, romance *is* the story. The plot of one of the biggest movies of all time was, essentially, "The Love Boat hits an iceberg." And the creative genius who brought a love story aboard the doomed *Titanic*, James Cameron, came back after a long hiatus to score an even bigger hit with a story about blue lovers who fight for environmental justice (*Avatar*). Even though Hollywood has refined the art of cinema romance, movies almost always neglect the deeper aspects of love. For lovers who stroll the silver screen, love equals sexual attraction, usually expressed through intense, seminude, lovemaking scenes. Fun to watch, perhaps, but not a good model of what constitutes love.[2]

Some Quick Thoughts

Certainly, passion plays an important part in many relationships, but it is in no wise the singular or even the most important element. Besides, not all "relationships" are sexual. We have children, extended families, friends, neighbors, work associates, social and business acquaintances, church and community members—none of whom share sexual intimacy with us, even though we may love them dearly. So if people spend so much time, money and energy on love, why do we get it wrong so often? Here are a few quick thoughts on popular misconceptions about love:

1) **Sensuality.** Much of what passes for love is sensual attraction and sexuality. In case you suspect I am advocating celibacy, let me hasten to say there is nothing wrong with sexual passion in romantic relationships. Few marriages last these days without

the partners being lovers too, but love involves much more than passion.

2) **In Love With Love.** Much of what passes for love is mere glamour. At the entry level of a romantic relationship, the lover is infatuated by the physical attractiveness of the other person. New love is a kind of madness, but infatuation is not love, and the rapture of a new relationship wears off eventually. Courtship ends, then what?

3) **Enabling/Dependencies.** Much of what passes for love is neurotic dependency. Some kinds of relationships are based on feelings of inadequacy. A song lyric made famous by Barbara Streisand goes:

> With one person, one very special person
> A feeling deep in your soul
> Says you were half,
> Now you're whole.[3]

What happens when two half-people find each other? The heart math doesn't add up to two whole people. If people establish relationships simply because they perceive something lacking that is provided by the other, they have not understood the message of Jesus Christ about the divine qualities within every human being. Only two whole people can truly love one another from their fullness; half-people are locked in enabling dependencies that limit the depth of their potential for intimacy and fulfillment.

4) **Fear of Loneliness.** Much of what passes for love is fear of loneliness. This is perfectly understandable, considering that many people today live with alienation in their everyday world. Until my generation, everyone pretty much knew their neighbors. My upbringing was like that; we lived in a row house in Reading, Pennsylvania, in the 1950s. My folks literally knocked on the wall to signal the neighbor lady to meet them in the yard

for conversation. We never had dinner at each other's homes, but we knew the people on both sides, across the street, and down the block by name. We also had blood relatives within an easy drive, city buses to travel to shopping areas downtown, and safe streets to walk day or night. Today in some communities, people feel imprisoned in their own homes.

Although the place where I live now has relatively little violent crime, I'm an example of this neo-local isolation too. I live far from family members, and I don't know my neighbors beyond a nod of recognition as they power-walk past on the tree-shaded street of our subdivision. In this isolated lifestyle, many people cling fiercely to their mates and expect the other person to fulfill all the functions that were previously provided by family, neighbors and a supportive, friendly community. No wonder some relationships fail to meet the needs of the partners.

5) **Ego, Jealousy and Selfishness.** Much of what passes for love is unbridled possessiveness. When I was a chaplain in the U.S. Army working with young married couples, I counseled young wives whose husbands got angry and abusive when other men merely noticed them. One man had jealous fits when the OB/GYN doctor performed a routine examination on his wife; another soldier took his wife's car keys when he went to work in the morning for fear she would sneak out during the day to meet some fantasized paramour. Because the military community is a cross section of middle class life, I suspect the problem of possessiveness is far more widespread than its presence among low-ranking soldiers. When young couples came to me for premarriage counseling, they often said their plans had accelerated when the soldier-fiancé received overseas reassignment orders. Some of these young people actually confessed that they wanted to get married now because they were afraid a separation would end their relationship.

Love, in its highest expression, is not possessive but liberating.

6) **Convenience.** Much of what passes for love is convenience, routine and economic comfort. Most of us know people who acknowledge they are in unsatisfying, loveless unions, yet their situations persist year after year because the partners would rather stay in their rut than risk changing their partners or improving the relationship.

So, What *Is* Love?

The obvious conclusion from these short summaries is that love isn't as easy as Hollywood pretends. But another point, seldom considered, is that love comes in more than one variety. The answer to "What is love?" depends on the context. We don't love our children the same way we love our country. We certainly don't love friends and neighbors the same way we love husbands and wives, unless we're behaving like characters in a tawdry novel. What about that obnoxious so-and-so at work? How about friends and family who have been cruel? How can we "love" people who are prejudiced against us, or members of a group that stands against everything we cherish?

When Jesus said, "Love your enemies," how far did he intend for that command to stretch? Some would say infinitely. Would Jesus insist that Jewish Holocaust survivors or freed slaves after the American Civil War were ethically required to love their persecutors? The question is not as clear as a first glimpse might suggest. Contemplating monstrous evil, such as the Holocaust or African slavery, could push thinking persons into a dark room. One can metaphysically understand "evil" as the absence of good, as it surely is, but studying the history of human inhumanity makes love of one's enemies a difficult goal to contemplate.

This chapter attempts to rediscover the underlying principles of Jesus about love by looking at four biblical-era words. It is a topic that clearly requires a separate book, perhaps several volumes. I shall attempt to do justice to the Christian understanding of love through brevity, trusting that others will follow to plumb its depths.

Four Kinds of Love

British Medieval literature scholar C.S. Lewis (1898-1963) wrote extensively on religion, and even when not specifically writing about his beliefs, a heavy measure of conservative Christian thought underscored Lewis's work. Some rather traditional themes about redemption and salvation dance through his science fiction novels and well-known fantasy series, *The Chronicles of Narnia*. Lewis is so deft at weaving theme and plot that most readers are unaware of the deeply pious sentiments that motivated Lewis to create a talking lion who dies to save the helpless from the powers of evil. Lewis's stories work at several levels—the Narnia Chronicles are, after all, children's books—and this ability to communicate deep ideas in layers of meaning is a tribute to his skill as an author.

One of Lewis's nonfiction works is a thin volume entitled *The Four Loves*. In this little book Lewis divides love into four categories: *affection, friendship, eros* (passion) and *charity* (self-giving). Lewis offers good insights into the complexities of human love and provides a revised vision of the traditional view of Divine Love. Yet I have always believed a complete reinterpretation of the word, based on the four biblical-era terms, would convey a more complete understanding of the vexing, beautiful, alluring power of love.

Some of my conclusions are very close to Lewis's views on love, others are not. For example, he does not elect to discuss *hesed*, dutiful love, and prefers to establish a separate category for *affection*. Furthermore, the notes from which this discussion proceeds come from preparation for a sermon series over 20 years ago, well before I had read Lewis's book. The similarity of my procedure—even the sequence which puts friendship, eros, and agape in that order—suggests I probably gleaned some "original" ideas from long-forgotten seminary lectures I attended in the 1970s, whose sources reach to Lewis's 1960 work. This chapter is a new statement, then, on the four kinds of love, and the reader can compare my work with Lewis to see how they differ and where they coincide.[4]

Four Words

Although the four words I will discuss are implicit in the teachings of Jesus, the Second Testament only puts one of them explicitly on his lips, and that connection is dubious. The problem is that Jesus likely spoke Aramaic, but the Christian Scriptures were written in Koine Greek, the common language of Hellenistic civilization. There is some possibility that Jesus was much more cosmopolitan than he is ordinarily pictured.

For a long time, scholars believed Jesus was from a sleepy backwater town in northern Palestine, but recent archaeological evidence suggests that the Roman city Sepphoris was within easy walking distance. Conceivably, Joseph of Nazareth took his son along to practice their carpentry trade in the bustling, expanding Roman town. Sepphoris boasted a Roman theater and an impressive array of tile mosaics, some now coming back into the light as archaeologists delicately sweep the ruins with fine hair brushes. Because of the practical need to do business in affluent, Roman Sepphoris, Jesus may have spoken conversational Greek, maybe even a little Latin. The Greek words explored in this chapter (*philia, eros, agape*) might have been well-known to him, because the concepts behind them certainly play major roles in his stories and teachings.

Very likely, Jesus knew the Hebrew word for love, *hesed*. Everyone familiar with the Gospels knows that Jesus read aloud in the synagogue, and scholars have noted that, as an adult Jew, he would have gone through the typical Hebrew education for his day. By the first century, Hebrew was a dead language that had to be studied so Jewish children could read the Bible, much as European youth for centuries studied ancient Greek and Latin to read Homer and Virgil in their original tongues. The adaptive Jewish community had produced Greek and Aramaic translations of the "Old Testament" for study and discussion, much as scholars translate the whole Bible into English versions today.

1. HESED: Love Is Steadfast and Loyal

In the Hebrew Bible, a common word for love is *hesed*, often translated "steadfast love." Well-known passages come to mind: "Praise the Lord! O give thanks to the Lord, for he is good; for his steadfast love endures forever!"[5]

A better translation for hesed is "faithful devotion."[6] Hesed is the kind of faithfulness that soldiers owe to their commanders, the respect children feel for their parents, and the allegiance citizens pay their country. It is grounded in duty, a whole-hearted devotion to someone or some cause that deserves unswerving loyalty.

Now there's a new concept: *Loyalty.* Are you old enough to remember loyalty? Elbert Hubbard put it this way:

> If you work for a man, for heaven's sake work for
> him: speak well of him and stand by the institu-
> tion he represents. Remember, an ounce of loy-
> alty is worth a pound of cleverness. If you must
> growl, condemn, and eternally find fault, why
> not resign your position? And when you are on
> the outside damn to your hearts content, but as

> long as you are part of the institution, do not con-
> demn it; if you do the first high wind that comes
> along will blow you away and you will never
> know why.[7]

Do you recall when working for someone meant working *for* someone? Nowadays, feeling a sense of ownership and pride in the business that employs you marks the employee as somewhat naive. Water cooler talk is seldom about how to make the company better, and discussions of the boss too often deteriorate into "ain't it awful" games, orgies of complaint with itemizations of managerial faults and abuses. Downsizings and seemingly arbitrary shuffling of personnel while corporate bosses take big bonuses doubtless have contributed to the dearth of hesed in the business world today.

Unfortunately, this is also true for the workplace in which the opposite reaction in workers should occur: the local congregation. Most clergy can recite horror stories about disloyal, backbiting, conspiratorial church members who seem to relish their role as tormentor of the minister. Seldom to one's face, of course. Clergy have told me they could deal with honest opposition, provided the aggravated member came to them directly and expressed concerns in the open. That almost never happens. Most people despise confrontation, so they follow the line of least resistance and air their grievances in private with other church members. This practice of triangulation, which author Gary Simmons calls *enlisting support*, may temporarily ventilate a person's frustrations, but it also begins to undermine group cohesion and works against loyalty to the minister, which clergy need for effective leadership. Consequently, when looking for a church assignment after a hiatus of several years, I told all the committees who interviewed me that, if I became their minister, I would never speak ill of them behind their backs and expected them to do likewise.

The natural tendency toward naysaying becomes deadly when coupled with disloyalty, and the combination has frustrated many a good ministry from developing a loving, open community under the vigorous leadership of a clergyperson who mutually trusts and is trusted by the people.

How About Patriotism?

Communities create their own compelling reasons for individual behavior. One of my seminary professors remarked that when he studied in Europe, quite a few years ago, he sent his son to German public school. It was raining the first day of class, so the lad wore a typical American school kid's yellow raincoat. Kids are kids all over the globe, so he was bitterly ridiculed for the cultural *faux pas*, and for not having a proper European backpack bookbag. Of course the American parents rushed out, bought the bookbag, and their son went smiling off to class the next day with no further incidents. Time passed quickly and the professor completed his studies and moved his young family back stateside. When the boy showed up at school with the European backpack and no raincoat ... well, you can guess the reaction from his American schoolmates. A new yellow raincoat solved the problem.

Who told the children to ostracize their chums for noncompliance with the dress code? No one, of course. There was no nefarious plot behind their corporate behavior; that is just an example of how cultural dynamics operate. I often experienced different twists on this groupthink phenomenon in my 10-year career as a teacher.

From the early 90s until the turn of the 21st century, when I returned to full-time ministry, I took an unofficial sabbatical from church leadership and taught middle school in the Georgia public schools. Middle schoolers, I learned, are a bundle of kinetic energy, wildly enthusiastic about everything. Then I moved to high school and discovered a different world. Those students had formulated and consolidated their values, and they were somewhat impervious to teacher suggestions.

Although my seniors displayed many admirable traits, there were a few areas where the generation gap (I was then in my early 50s) created problems for me. Patriotism—or the lack of it—for example. Disturbingly, most of my 11th grade homeroom students flatly refused to say the "Pledge of Allegiance" each morning. When I asked them why, I got mumbles instead of answers. Not that they had any political or ethical objections to the pledge, of course. Their silence was social, not an act of protest. In what was probably an excessive use of teacher-power, I detained a band of 11th graders after the bell and refused to let them go to first-period class until they told me why they would not say the pledge. One young man finally blurted, "Because I don't have to!" Nobody else said the pledge, and he didn't want to stand out. Bottom line on why this group of high school students wouldn't pledge allegiance to the flag?

It just wasn't cool.

In fairness to the kids, this was in the late 1990s, before 9/11 reawakened American patriotism. The lesson I learned that morning is still valid. Culture often determines values, and when it comes to religious values, they should be examined in the light generated during an interactive dialogue between embedded theology and the biblical-theological Jesus.

What would Jesus do about war, and how much would he have advocated patriotism? His recorded remarks, if they are historical, suggest a degree of loyalty to the social order as long as it does not compel individuals to violate their higher calling as children of a loving God.

That definitely would not be cool.

Remembering Loyalty

Eastern mystics have long understood the need for loyalty—to spiritual leaders like gurus, sages and teachers, but also representatives of the social order. In the closing decades of the 20th century, some Westerners laughed at TV images of the Japanese soldiers who stayed in hiding on remote Pacific islands until decades after WWII had ended, but no one laughed in Japan. Asians understand loyalty. If you've read James Clavel's novel *Shogun*, you know that the Samurai code of honor, *Bushido*, rested squarely on the principle of hesed. Samurai would promptly take their own lives if ordered by their liege lord. Dishonor required defeated armies to commit *seppuku*, or *hara-kiri* (literally, "belly cutting"), a form of ritualized suicide. This demonstrated their fidelity to Bushido, which in the mythology of Shinto guaranteed their rebirth as Samurai. Modern Japanese workers seldom kill themselves when their corporations are swallowed up by hostile mergers, but bosses nevertheless expect fierce loyalty of employees, who can usually count on working for the same company for life.

Where the principle of hesed is applied, relationships firm up. Dependable love reshapes the dynamics of collegiality, co-working, partnership, friendship, marriage and family. An argument could be made that today, especially in the realm of romantic love, a little stubborn loyalty wouldn't be a bad thing.

2. PHILIA: Love Is Friendly

Loyalty alone is not enough to form a high theology of love. So add the next element, a Greek term found in the Second Testament, *philia*, which can be translated "friendship." Before the feminist revolution, men called it "brotherly love." The term philia is found only once in the Second Testament at James 4:4, and even there it appears to have an uncomplimentary context:

"Do you not know that *friendship* with the world is enmity with God?" The word itself simply means "friendship" or "brotherly love." Philadelphia, the "city of brotherly love," was founded by Quakers.

What Does Friendship/Brotherly Love Imply?

Equality. Friendships are mutual relationships.

Trust. Friends are loyal and faithful.

Free choice. We don't choose family, but we choose friends.

Enjoyment. Friends are people with whom we associate freely because we like being with them.

Reciprocity. Friends will do things for us, and we for them.

Doubtless this war-plagued world could use a lot more philia. Friends get along by learning that anybody can have a bad day, even the people we like best. Some kinds of behavior step so far out there that even a friend must call it wrong.

This was surely the case when four white Los Angeles policemen beat up Rodney King, a black taxicab driver who was allegedly high on drugs at the time of his arrest. When the brutal beating was caught on videotape and played repeatedly on all news networks, many people who saw the video—myself included—thought it showed a disgraceful abuse of police powers. A predominantly white jury nevertheless acquitted the policemen. In the aftermath of the acquittal, racially motivated riots broke out across the country. The worst violence occurred in Los Angeles itself, with 55 deaths, 2,383 injuries, more than 7,000 fire responses, and 3,100 plus businesses vandalized by angry mobs. Total damage in the Los Angeles riots was in excess of $1 billion.

In the midst of this ferocity, a plainly bewildered Rodney King came to the microphone and asked the nation, perhaps the world, a profound question:

> People, I just want to say, you know, can't we all
> just get along?[8]

His question was motivated by a spirit not unlike philia, a simple desire to coexist in a friendly world, regardless of the momentary evils that might spring from the combination of human free will and spiritual immaturity. Although it was plainly wrong for those policemen to beat and abuse Rodney King, an offense compounded by their acquittal by an all-white jury, the rioting in the aftermath of the verdict only expanded the tragedy and further alienated black and white communities. Rodney King's plaintive question lingers to this day as one of the few good legacies in this sorry affair: "Can't we all just get along?"

The spirit of philia is still needed in this world.

3. EROS: Love Is Appreciation

The word *eros* is not specifically found in the Second Testament, although it is implied in several places. Usually, it is thought of as sexual love; the word "erotic" comes from eros. However, the meaning goes much deeper. Eros does denote sexual desire, passionate aspiration and sensual longing, but it also can mean the upward longing for the eternal and the divine. Generally, eros refers to the attraction felt for some beautiful or desirous object, idea or event. Although the word is not found in the Bible, its influence is everywhere. For example, the *Song of Solomon* is clearly meant as a hymn to erotic love.

Hebrew consciousness struggled mightily with its erotic side. Documents found among the Dead Sea Scrolls refer to a fine levied for public nakedness. Biblical rules included prohibitions against the following: sex during menstruation, men and women wearing each other's clothing, any kind of public nakedness (including exposure of the middle of the body), all forms of lesbianism and homosexuality, a woman intervening in a quarrel between her husband and another man by seizing the opponent's genitals, and worshipping through the cult of temple prostitutes. It is interesting to note that prostitution for money itself is never explicitly outlawed. All the condemnations are leveled at so-called "sacred prostitutes" of the various non-Hebrew temples. Of course, all forms of adultery were punishable by death.

What was the definition of adultery? It was a sexual act committed between a married woman and someone who was not her husband. Note that a married man having sex with a single woman was not considered adultery; that was fornication, a lesser sin. Jesus leveled the playing field somewhat when he told the crowds that even *thinking* about adultery is tantamount to doing it, so they had no reason to act so high and mighty.

Eros also referred to appreciation of beauty. To gaze at a magnificent statue was eros; to be carried away by a glorious sunset on the sea was eros. Anything that brought delight through the senses could be understood as eros.

How do the various Jesuses of Scripture view this type of love? Surprisingly, the Bible describes rather unanimously a man who enjoyed life and exhibited a love of good things. He took pleasure in the perfumed oil a woman massaged into his feet; he enjoyed partying, making good wine at marriage feast at Cana. He went to dinner parties, drank wine, consorted with females, and generally had a good time whenever he could. In fact, Jesus was apparently known for partying so much that his detractors called him a "glutton and a drunkard."[9]

One might infer his attitude toward eros was that passion for life is good; life's good pleasures are to be embraced, not shunned. Aesthetics is important, because beauty is a gift of God. Sensuality-sexuality is the entry-level of romantic relationships. The Talmud—that great compendium of Jewish commentary on Scripture, and commentaries on the commentaries—says there will come a time when "a person is to give an accounting of everything he saw, but did not enjoy."[10] It is not difficult to imagine Jesus encouraging his followers to enjoy the world and its beauty, because *not* to do so is sinful.

Was Jesus Married?

Recent theories have floated around about Jesus and Mary Magdalene having an intimate relationship. Bishop John Shelby Spong speculates that perhaps Magdalene was his wife. This interesting question will probably never be answered, but a sexually active Jesus is nothing to fear unless there is something inherently dirty about sex itself. Whereas the by-products of human sexuality are ritually unclean in Hebrew thought—semen, menstrual flow, etc.—sex itself is a *mitzvah*, a blessing, which is allowed and even encouraged on Sabbath. In fact, nothing in Jewish law or the life and teachings of Rabbi Yeshua suggests anything like abhorrence for normal pleasures. If Jesus was the Messiah, he was unquestionably an erotic savior in the full sense of the words.

4. AGAPE: Love Is Compassion—Selfless, Altruistic and Counterintuitive

The word favored by NT writers when they speak of love is agape. It actually means *selfless love,* the kind that puts the other person first. Perhaps the most powerful biblical example of agape is the story told by Luke that has come to be called the Parable of the Good Samaritan. I discuss this parable at length in the next essay, but suffice it to say that the Samaritan had no motivation for personal gain in his actions of merciful kindness to the wounded traveler. The unconscious man wasn't even able to say "Thank you" to this unknown benefactor. The Samaritan, who was a member of a despised ethnic minority, exceeded all reasonable expectations, not only treating the victim's wounds but carrying him to an inn, paying for his room and board, and offering more compensation if the money he provided ran out before the victim recovered. *That is agape.* It goes the second, third and fourth mile, not for personal reward but simply because it is the loving thing to do.

The Good Samaritan story calls for humanity to see that other humans have the right to exist and be regarded with dignity. Apparently, the first-century church believed the heart of the Gospel was this understanding of selfless love. Agape is more than a moral suggestion; John gives Jesus' followers a "new commandment":

> That you love (agapate) one another. Just as I have loved you, you also should love one another. By this everyone will know that you are my disciples, if you have love for one another.[11]

Remember the Robbers?

It is important to recognize that agape as demanded by the biblical Jesus—i.e., all people have the right to unqualified acceptance and positive esteem—seems to run afoul of the natural order. In nature there are no *rights*, only *powers*. It is a giant leap forward when a species of omnivores, like *Homo sapiens*, accords rights of existence to its own members and begins to hesitate before attacking, killing and eating the stray who has wandered off course. An ocean of blood separates "Live and let live" from the more primordial question "What's in it for me?" Tolerance of diversity is the moral equivalent of coming down from the trees and walking upright. And, in the social evolution of our race, the movement from cooly tolerating outsiders to embracing the stranger in an act of altruism constitutes a leap from the forest floor to the stars.

Although it may seem counterintuitive for a species member to seek the health and well-being of his rivals, these altruistic values are essential building blocks for all complex societies. Just as the Lakota needed to trust that the hunter sleeping in the next lodge would not steal his horses and kill him in the night, so nation-states need to know that the default behavior of their economic and political adversaries in other lands is not opportunistic aggression but peaceful, commercial competition. This tolerance is based on mutual need, but Jesus and other great teachers of humanity have long called for humanity to move beyond tolerance to a place where respect yields to mutual admiration and trust. The human race still has its challenges: some people have not yet come down from the trees or given up tribal warfare.

The Good Samaritan is the model to emulate, but there are plenty of robbers on the road who have not learned this lesson yet, as 9/11 shows. Peaceful, kindly humans must continue to help the victims out of the ditch, but someone has to deal with the robbers or the victimization will continue. One could argue a variety of ways—ranging from retribution to reconciliation—to make the metaphorical highways of life safe from robbers, but the point here is that nothing in the teaching of Jesus requires denial of the problem or capitulation to helpless suffering. Tough love can still be an expression of agape. If you doubt this, meditatively visit the Jerusalem Temple and ask the moneychangers.

Applications of Agape

Agape applies to all kinds of relationships, friend-to-friend, person-to-acceptable co-worker, even person-to-obnoxious jerk.

In her book *Seeing Children, Seeing God*, Pamela Couture rightly indicates that caring actions must be independent of the response of the person served: "True generosity continues even when others do not respond as we would like; otherwise, our kind actions were bait, rather than generosity."[12] This sounds like Charles Fillmore:

> Let us give as God gives, unreservedly, and with no thought of return, making no mental demands for recompense on those who have received from us. A gift with reservations is not a gift; it is a bribe.[13]

When a person acts from heartfelt consciousness, it does not matter whether the act is acknowledged or not. Perhaps, in certain circumstances, a thankless rebuff is more conducive to spiritual growth than a hug and a kiss, although the latter certainly feels better.

Love Prescription: What Is Needed in Relationships?

Less Eros and more Agape. It's not that eros is bad, but rather the sensual-attractive side of relationships has been overplayed. This is so self-evident in Western society that the case need not be explicitly stated; everyone old enough to surf the Internet or operate a TV remote knows that Western culture wallows in sensual-sexual imagery.

Less Hollywood and more Jerusalem. Perhaps this idea is contained in the first point above. Glamour is alluring; action-adventure stories where evil is destroyed in the last moments of the movie provide a sense of satisfaction. Yet the world is infinitely more complex than two teams of super attractive athletes squaring off in a battle between good and evil. Who were the good guys and bad guys in the biblical stories? Were the Romans evil, or the Jews? One could understand the Second Testament setting as a struggle between imperial, enslaving Rome and freedom-loving Israel; yet the same story can be cast as a battle between urbane, progressive Hellenistic civilization and fanatical religious terrorists, with Jewish zealots playing the role of Al-Qaeda in the first century. Certainly there have been times when one side represents monstrous "evil," such as the Nazis, but most conflicts have been less black and white. Rodney King's hard question should be set in the stained glass windows of every church in the world: *Can't we all just get along?*

Less emphasis on attractiveness and more on compatibility. This is especially true for romantic relationships, but it probably applies equally to all forms of human interaction. In most human cultures, pretty people have always had both an advantage and disadvantage. The advantage is obvious: physically attractive people are simply treated better in almost every circumstance. This has been shown in study after study. A stunningly attractive woman once confessed to me, as her minister, that she didn't know what people actually thought about her, because they always related to her physical beauty and not her ideas, character or personality.

A good measure of philia. Mutuality and reciprocity; each side gives more than 50 percent. The best kind of relationships share and allow for the occasional episode of temporary insanity in others.

Resolution of conflicts without winning or losing. Quarrels between intimates or strangers can best be resolved by looking for solutions rather than identifying villains. Agape represents the hope for better human relationships; each participant wishes good will for all and is willing to strive selflessly to achieve healing of the nations.

Imago Dei: Jesus, You and Me

Jesus was a first-century Jew, and one can find elements of all four kinds of love in the rabbinic literature of his day. Christianity hardly invented selfless love; the lives of Hebrew prophets displayed marked tendencies toward sacrificial devotion to God and the people. What the Jesus Event provides is a rallying point, a demonstration of divine love walking among us, an example of what *Imago Dei* looks like as it strolls the marketplace of life. As mentioned in previous chapters, many Christians find unique divinity in Jesus, a quality unshared by the masses who live and love and sin and struggle.

Yet, metaphysically speaking, I cannot see anything in Jesus that is not present in you and me. Embellished with miracle stories, perhaps he walks across the lake a bit more skillfully than I do, but run the biblical tales through Bultmann's program of demythologizing and what appears is a human striving to express the divine within, just like everyone else. The difference seems to be that Jesus succeeded to such a degree that his life has become a paradigm of what everyone could be. He shows the way; hence a good title for Jesus in the 21st century might be the Way Shower.

Doubtless there are many more ways to look at love than the four discussed here. I have not considered family love, healthy self-love or the undeniable love people feel for pets. The life and teachings of Jesus can provide good starting points to have those conversations, and many more.

New Downloads Forthcoming

The model of divine love expressed by Jesus will doubtless continue to be a subject of discussion as *Homo sapiens* progresses toward what has been called global consciousness. As humanity through time has learned more about what it means to be human, we have repudiated previously normative practices such as geno-cide, aggressive territorial warfare, slavery, politically enforced racism and the subjugation of women. Now a growing consensus is calling for an extension of human consciousness once more, to excise homophobia and ethnocentric nationalism; to protect the earth and its resources; to expand democratic freedoms and pro-mote equal justice under humane laws; to provide free public education, universal health care and economic opportunity to all levels of human society in every part of the world. Jesus never addressed many of these issues because they were not relevant to his era. However, the Jesus model of selfless love, agape, applies everywhere all the time.

If the present work says anything, it's that Jesus is alive and available to everyone today through the ongoing, creative inter-action between the biblical, traditional and contemporary sources of information about him. Jesus 2.1 will continue to enlighten and uplift those who choose to turn to him, and when the next generation or the generation after that needs to rethink the model for its age, there will doubtless be a Jesus 2.2, Jesus 3.0, and onward. This ongoing process of reinterpretation, adaptation and integration of the Way Shower of humanity will continue until we reach the omega point of our species, or until the forces of evolu-tion trigger the arrival of a new Jesus figure for whatever crea-tures exist in those distant times. Certainly, whether human or descended from humans, or having arisen from some new species, as long as they are mortal they will need to hear anew the ancient word of the Lord from all the Jesuses yet unborn.

The Water-Walker
by
Thomas Shepherd*

When Jesus walked upon the sea
He turned His head and called to me,
"Come out and join Me on the waves!"
"No, thank You, Sir. I'm not that brave."

Don't glare at me—I would've gone,
But I had my good sandals on,
And though Lord Jesus gets my vote,
I'd rather cast it from the boat.

He laughed and slid a watery hill,
"I don't know why you linger still;
The boat is safer—do you think?
Bad news, My friend, it might soon sink.

"And if you want to walk away,
Bravely you must seize the day
And leave the safety of the boat
To follow Me and stay afloat."

"Uh—Jesus? Must I risk my neck?
Can't I just send in my check?
It looks too scary on the sea,
I'll stay aboard and pray for Thee.

"Besides, if the truth were told
It's not just that I'm never bold,
I have my doubts, suspicions too.
In fact, I don't believe in You.

"I've read the Greek philosophers
And frankly I've decided, Sir,
That Plato was a smarter knave,
He'd never try to walk on waves.

"Heraclitus gave good advice—
He'd never step on a river twice,
And Socrates was martyred too—
Not just some overzealous Jew.

"So trot on home across the sea
Without another thought of me,
I'm quite content—You need not save—
I am not threatened by the waves."

He smiled and walked away alone,
The sea got calm and I sailed home.
But now and then, when rolls the sea
And troubles crash like waves o'er me,
I wonder what my life would be
If I'd gone walking on the sea.

*Originally published in *Unity Magazine*.

ENDNOTES

Foreword

1   *http://www.creeds.net/ancient/nicene.htm* (accessed 05-12-2010).

2   "One Solitary Life," blank verse poem/short essay often attributed to James Allan Francis, available online at *http://www.associatedcontent.com/article/660641/one_solitary_life. html* (accessed 05-10-2010).

3   *http://www.messiahcd.com/Information/about_The_ Messiah/about_the_messiah.html*

Introduction

1   Harry Emerson Fosdick, *The Living of These Days* (New York: Harper and Brothers, 1956), 230.

2   Christology encompasses theological and historical studies about Jesus Christ.

3   Albert Schweitzer, quoted in Jaroslav Pelikan, *Jesus Through the Centuries* (New York: History Book Club, 1996), 2.

4   Fosdick, 230.

Chapter 1: First Thoughts

1   Dr. Robert Martin, Handout on "Writing" provided to D.Min. Class, Saint Paul School of Theology, 2006.

2   "One Solitary Life," poem, available online at *http://www. geocities.com/onesolitarylife_isJesus/Lord-and-Savior.html* (accessed 09-12-09).

3   "The Politics of Christianity: A Talk With Elaine Pagels," unsigned article based on 07-17-03 interview with Elaine

Pagels. www.edge.com. John Brockman, ed., available online at *http://www.edge.org/3rd_culture/pagels03/pagels_index.html* (accessed 02-04-08).

4 Rev. Ed Hird, "Jesus Loves Me, This I know," *Deep Cove Crier*, November 1993, available online at *http://www3.telus.net/st_simons/cr9311.htm* (accessed 01-24-08).

5 Douglas John Hall (Emeritus Professor of Christian Theology, McGill University), "Who Can Say It as It Is? Karl Barth on the Bible," (Montreal, Canada: Department of Religion, University of Calgary, March 8, 2004), 6. Available online at *http://www.ucalgary.ca/christchair/files/christchair/Hall_BarthOnBible.pdf* (accessed 11-16-09).

6 "Cafeteria Christianity," *Concerned Catholics,* available online at *http://www.concernedcatholics.org/cafeteria.htm* (accessed 02-02-08).

7 John Shelby Spong, *The Sins of Scripture* (New York: HarperCollins, 2005), 18.

8 Galatians 5:22: "The fruit of the Spirit is love, joy, peace, patience, kindness, generosity, faithfulness, gentleness, and self-control."

9 Robert W. Funk, *Honest to Jesus* (New York: HarperSan Fransisco, 1996), 42.

10 Albert Schweitzer, *The Quest of the Historical Jesus,* tr. William Montgomery (New York: Macmillan, 1961), 4.

Chapter 2: An Ordinary Man Who Changed the World

1 Matthew Fox, unpublished notes from lecture at Unity Institute, 06-21-06.

2 Funk, 37.

3 Jay Wells, quoted in Mandy Crow, "Antidote to Ministry Frustration Is in the Bible," available online at *http://www. pastors.com/blogs/ministrytoolbox/archive/2002/09/12/Antidote-to-ministry-frustration-is-in-the-Bible.aspx* (accessed 01-27-08).

4 Richard Bach, *Jonathan Livingston Seagull: A Story* (New York: Scribner, 1970), 83. (Parenthesis added).

5 Ibid., 84.

6 Alfred H. Ackley (music and lyrics), Hymn: "He Lives!" available online at *http://www.tagnet.org/digitalhymnal/en/dh251.html*

7 Rudolf Bultmann, *Kerygma and Myth,* available online at *http://www.religion-online.org/showchapter.asp?title=431&C=292* (accessed 02-13-10).

8 Matthew 5:48.

9 2 Corinthians 5:19.

Chapter 3: Jesus 2.1—Interactive, Postmodern Paradigm

1 Friedrich Nietzsche, *Genealogy of Morals, 3rd Essay, Part 12.* Available online at *http://nietzsche.classicauthors.net/ GenealogyMorals/GenealogyMorals55.html* (accessed 06-30-10).

Chapter 4: Dream a Little Dream With Me

1 John Shelby Spong, e-mail newsletter, *A New Christianity for a New World: Bishop John Shelby Spong on the News and the Christian Faith,* Q&A for 9/25/08.

2 *http://www.heroesofhistory.com/page63.html*

3 Habakkuk 1:4.

4 Romans 12:2.

5 Dietrich Bonhoeffer, *The Cost of Discipleship* (New York: MacMillan, 1963), 47.

6 Hans Küng, *On Being a Christian* (New York: Pocket Books, 1978), 123.

7 Ralph Waldo Emerson, available online at *http://www.christians.org/command/com02.htm*

8 Ibid.

9 Paul Tillich, quoted in John A.T. Robinson, *Honest to God* (Philadelphia: SCM Press, 1963), 22.

10 Ibid.

11 Matthew 10:37-39 (*Revised Standard Version*).

12 Matthew 13:54-57.

Chapter 5: Practical Christianity, Metaphysics and Theology

1 Anthony Flew, *A Dictionary of Philosophy* (New York: St. Martin's Press, 1979), 212-13.

2 Ibid., 213.

3 Charles Fillmore, *The Revealing Word* (Unity Village, Mo.: Unity Books, 1979), 132.

4 Alcoholics Anonymous Sayings, available online at *http://www.winternet.com/~terrym/aphorisms.html* (accessed 04-20-07).

5 Myrtle Fillmore, *Myrtle Fillmore's Healing Letters,* ed. Francis W. Foulkes (Unity Village, Mo.: Unity Books, 1954), 132.

6 Thomas W. Shepherd, *Glimpses of Truth* (Carol City, Fla.: UFBL Press, 2000), 25.

7 Marcus J. Borg and N.T. Wright, *The Meaning of Jesus: Two Visions* (New York: HarperCollins, 2000), 17.

8 Anthropologically speaking, one could argue that, in a bizarre way, this makes Satanism a misshapen form of Christianity, an idea likely to make partisans in both camps shudder.

9 Howard W. Stone, Harold and James O. Duke, *How to Think Theologically*, 2nd ed. (Minneapolis, Minn.: Fortress Press, 2006), 13 ff.

10 Shepherd, 132.

11 Stone and Duke, 43ff.

12 Ibid., 34-38.

13 C. Austin Miles, "In the Garden" (1946), lyrics available online at *http://www.bcpl.net/~bbengies/PAGE20.HTML#IN*

Chapter 6: Jesus and the Christ: The New Paradigm

1 Marcus J. Borg, *The Heart of Christianity* (San Francisco, Calif.: HarperSanFransisco, 2003), xii.

2 Ibid.

3 Ibid., 28.

4 The Athanasian Creed, Proposition 24.

5 Definition of Fundamentalism, Point 4, World Congress of Fundamentalists, 1976, available online at *http://www.wayoflife.org/otimothy/tl050006.htm*

6 Pagels, "Politics of Christianity."

7 For full text, see Luke 10:25-28.

8 James 2:14-18 (*Today's English Version*).

9 Ibid., 2:19.

10 Borg, 31-34.

11 Matthew 14:31.

12 Borg, 33.

13 Matthew 16:4.

14 Acts 1:6.

15 *http://www.worldtrans.org* (accessed 02-13-10).

16 Borg, 34-36. For a deeper discussion on three choices people make—to believe the world is hostile, indifferent or nurturing—see *The Responsible Self* by H. Richard Niebuhr (San Francisco: Harper and Row, 1963), especially pp. 139-45.

Chapter 7: The Vantage Point of History

1 John Shelby Spong, "Q&A" Newsletter for 09-04-08.

Chapter 8: The Apostles

1 Funk, 37.

2 The Greek version of the Jewish Scriptures, known as the Septuagint or *LXX*, was the primary Bible read by Jews in Diaspora. When Second Testament authors quote the Jewish scriptures, they invariably quote the *LXX* instead of making a fresh translation from the Hebrew. This becomes important when *LXX* and the Hebrew Scriptures offer significantly different wording in several places, because Christian writers obediently followed the *LXX*. Thus we have a word which means "young woman" in Hebrew which is rendered "virgin" in the "New" Testament, because the author followed the Greek *LXX* translation of Isaiah. If the original Christian documents had been in Aramaic, this flagrant plagiarizing of the Greek *LXX* probably would not have happened.

3 Psalm 23:5.

4 Jonathan Marcus, "Secularism vs. Orthodox Judaism," *BBC News Online*, 22 April, 1998, available online at *http://news.bbc.co.uk/2/hi/events/israel_at_50/israel_today/81033.stm* (accessed 10-31-09).

5 The anglicized name *Jesus* (Greek, *Iesous*, Latin, *Ieusus*) is based upon *Yeshua*, or *Joshua*, which means *God delivers*. It is probably no coincidence that the Christian answer to the problem is

found through a man called Jesus Christ, i.e., "the deliverer who is anointed by God."

6   Funk, 228.

7   Luke 1:41.

8   *The Clementine Recognitions* 1:54.8, The Pseudo-Clementine writings; available online at the Australian Ejournal of Theology, National School of Theology, Australian Catholic University. *http://dlibrary.acu.edu.au/research/theology/ejournal/ aejt_4/coloe.htm*

9   Funk, 127.

10 Acts 1:6.

11 Mark 14:61-62.

12 Luke 24:31-32.

13 *http://www.nakedauthors.com/2007/08/conspiracy-theory.html* (accessed 02-13-10).

14 See: Matthew 28:11-15; Luke 24:36-42; John 21:9-15.

Chapter 9: The Self-Appointed Apostle Paul

1   John Shelby Spong, *Rescuing the Bible From Fundamentalism* (New York: HarperCollins, 1992), 82.

2   Funk, *Honest to Jesus*, 37.

3   Ibid., 39.

4   Spong, 105.

5   Philippians 2:10-11.

6   John Dominic Crossan, *Jesus: A Revolutionary Biography* (New York: HarperCollins, 1994), 164.

7. 1 Corinthians 15:12-19.

8   1 Corinthians 15:3.

9 Romans 5:8-10.

10 José Ignacio Cabezón, *Buddhist-Christian Studies* 19.1 (1999): 51-61, University of Hawaii, available online at *http://muse. jhu.edu/demo/buddhist-christian_studies/v019/19.1 cabezon.html* (accessed 06-16-08).

11 Lewis E. Jones, "There is Power in the Blood" (1899), available online at *http://www.cyberhymnal.org/htm/t/h/therepow.htm* (accessed 02-13-10).

12 Marjoe Gornter, *Marjoe*, quoted by unnamed reviewer at movie review site *http://www99.epinions.com/review/ Marjoe_Marjoe_Gortner/content_405715586692* (accessed 10-31-09).

13 John 1:29. It is John the Baptist who pronounces this title, at least according to the partisan record of the fourth Gospel.

14 2 Corinthians 5:19.

15 1 Corinthians 8:13.

16 1 Corinthians 15:4-8.

17 1 Corinthians 15:6.

18 1 Corinthians 15:17.

19 Crossan, 166.

20 Ibid., 165.

21 This comment was often made in seminary courses that the author attended in the 1970s. Even then, the idea was not presented as particularly new or revolutionary.

22 1 Corinthians 1:22-24.

23 1 Corinthians 7:10-12, 15.

24 Philippians 2:5-8.

25 Philippians 2:9-11.

26 Romans 6:4-5, 11.

27 Pierre Teilhard de Chardin, *http://www.turrisfortis.com/words.html* (accessed 11-06-09).

28 I have discussed the concept of kenosis as normative at some length in my previous book, *Glimpses of Truth* (UFLB Press, 2000).

Chapter 10: Crash Course in Christological Controversies

1 Hans Küng, *On Being a Christian* (New York: Doubleday, 1984), 125.

2 For a more extensive discussion of this subject, see my essay, "Why We're Not a Cult," which is an appendix to the third edition of my book *Friends in High Places*.

3 Alister E. McGrath, *Christian Theology* (Oxford: Blackwell Publishers, 1999), 18.

4 Arthur Cushman McGiffert, *A History of Christian Thought*, Vol. 1. (New York: Charles Scribner's Sons, 1960), 244.

5 Richard P. McBrien, ed., *The HarperCollins Encyclopedia of Catholicism* (San Francisco: HarperCollins, 1995), 447b.

6 McGiffert, 244.

7 Alister E. McGrath, *The Christian Theology Reader* (Oxford: Blackwell Publishers, 1995), 176.

8 Eric Bazilian; *www.lyricsondemand.com/onehitwonders/ifgodwasoneofuslyrics.html* (accessed 02-13-10).

9 John 10:27-30.

10 McGrath, *Theology Reader*, 139.

11 McGiffert, 248.

12 McGrath, *Christian Theology*, 333-34.

13 Ibid., 333.

14 Ibid., 334-35.

[15] McGrath, *Theology Reader*, 139.

[16] "The Nicene Creed," *Book of Worship for the US Armed Forces* (Washington, DC: US Government Printing, 1974), 579.

Chapter 11: Jesus Christ for Today

[1] Spong, *Bishop Spong Q&A, Online Newsletter* (05-25-05).

[2] Bruce Bawer, *Stealing Jesus* (New York: Three Rivers Press, 1997), 41.

[3] Mark 14:32-36.

[4] Matthew 26:38-39.

[5] Luke 22:41-44.

[6] Luke 1:1.

[7] John 18:1-3, 10-11.

[8] Funk, *Honest to Jesus*, 11.

[9] John Shelby Spong, *Rescuing the Bible From Fundamentalism* (New York: HarperCollins, 1992), 207. If the reader is interested in which passages of Scripture were most probably spoken by the historical Jesus, scholars of the Jesus Seminar have infamously established principles to evaluate which Second Testament sayings Jesus probably said. See their website at *http://virtualreligion.net/forum/*

[10] Jack Canfield and Mark Victor Hansen, *Chicken Soup for the Soul* (New York: Health Communications, Inc., 1993), 69-70.

[11] Eric Butterworth, *Discover the Power Within You, 20th Anniversary Edition* (New York: Harper Collins, 1992), xv. Also found in the 40th anniversary edition, published in partnership with Unity House.

Chapter 12: Six Reasons to Follow Jesus

1 Mark 6:4-5.

2 Harry Emerson Fosdick, quoted in Bruce Bawer, *Stealing Jesus* (New York: Three Rivers Press, 1997), 115.

3 Marcus J. Borg, *Jesus: A New Vision* (New York: HarperCollins, 1991), 191.

4 Funk, 10-11.

5 Matthew 6:6.

6 *Microsoft Encarta 2000 Encyclopedia*, CD Rom, *Pre-Columbian Religions, Part IV A, Aztec Religion—The Nature of the Universe*.

7 Henry Van Etten, *George Fox and the Quakers*, tr. E. Kelvin Osborn (New York: Harper Torchbooks, 1959), 9.

8 *Easton's Bible Dictionary* in *The Ultimate Bible Suite* CD Rom (Olympia, Wa.: Strategic Product Marketing, Inc., 1997).

9 Marcus J. Borg, *Meeting Jesus Again for the First Time* (New York: HarperCollins, 1995), 35-36.

10 Mark 11:20-24.

11 John 8:15.

12 Spong, *Rescuing*, 21-22.

13 Romans 5:8.

14 Ralph Waldo Emerson, "The Divinity School Address," in *Three Prophets of Religious Liberalism*, ed. Conrad Wright (Boston: Beacon Press, 1961), 96-97.

15 Matthew 5:13-16.

16 Robert Schuller, speaking during the *Hour of Power Broadcast 01/21/01*, on the mission of the Crystal Cathedral.

17 1 Corinthians 15:54-55.

Chapter 13: Jesus Christ and Self-Esteem

1 See Jennings quote in North Peninsula Unity Center website: *http://www.northpeninsulaunitycenter.org/Principles/Unity_Basic_ Principle_5.asp* (accessed February 1, 2010).

2 John B. Noss, in Thomas Shepherd's unpublished student class notes of a lecture, Fall 1975.

3 John B. Noss, *Man's Religions* (New York: Macmillan, 1974), 162.

4 Johnnie Colemon, *"Namaskar!"* in *Daily Inspiration for Better Living* magazine (Carol City, Fla.: UFBL Publications, March 2001), 3.

5 Mark 12:35-36.

6 Bahá'u'lláh, *"The Tablet of Ahmad,"* in *Bahá'í Prayers* (Wilmette, Ill.: Bahá'í Publishing Trust, 1991), 211.

7 Shepherd, *Glimpses*, 13.

8 1-800-NOW-PRAY (1-800-669-7729).

9 *http://www.quotationspage.com/quote/31650.html* (accessed 08-02-08).

10 Matthew 5:13-16.

11 James S. Hewett, *Illustrations Unlimited* (Wheaton, Ill.: Tyndale House Publishers, Inc, 1988), 246-247.

Chapter 14: Jesus Christ and Relationships

1 John 15:12.

2 *Avatar* is probably an exception to this rule. The love between the hero and heroine develops over time and runs deeper than typical Hollywood romances based on sexual attraction alone.

3 "People," lyrics by Bob Merrill, available online at *http:// www.seeklyrics.com/lyrics/Barbra-Streisand/People-From- Broadway-Musical.html* (accessed 01-24-08).

4 C.S. Lewis, *The Four Kinds of Love* (New York: Harcourt Brace, 1991).

5 Psalm 106:1.

6 Sheila E. McGinn, "Glossary: Basic Terms for Biblical Study," available online at *http://www.jcu.edu/Bible/BibleIntroReadings/ Glossary.htm* (accessed 02-13-10).

7 Elbert Hubbard (1856-1915), quoted at www.quoteland.com, available online at *http://forum.quoteland.com/1/OpenTopic? a=tpc&s=586192041&f=099191541&m=6531055101* (accessed 01-19-08).

8 Rodney King Home Page, *http://lsnhs.leesummit.k12.mo.us/ dtwp/spring07/historical/hour5/historical_bradr/index.htm* (accessed 05-15-07).

9 Matthew 11:19.

10 Talmud Study Website, *http://web.me.com/tehart/Jurassic_Rants/ Books_and_Rants/Entries/2009/8/29_The_Talmud.html* (accessed 02-13-10).

11 John 13:34-35.

12 Pamela D. Couture, *Seeing Children, Seeing God* (Nashville, Tenn.: Abingdon, 2005), 57.

13 Charles R. Fillmore, *Dynamics for Living* (Unity Village, Mo.: Unity Books, 1967), 208.

About the Author

The Rev. Dr. Thomas W. Shepherd is a retired U.S. Army Chaplain who has served religious communities around the world for more than 30 years in the clergy. Before studying for the ministry, he flew medical evacuation helicopters in Vietnam, earning two Distinguished Flying Crosses, Air Medal, Purple Heart, and the Vietnamese Cross of Gallantry. Shepherd holds a B.S.Ed. from the University of Idaho, Master of Divinity from Lancaster Theological Seminary, and Doctor of Ministry from Saint Paul School of Theology. He has served as assistant executive director of the Universal Foundation for Better Living and as senior minister of Unity churches in Georgia, South Carolina, and California.

In 2005, Shepherd became de facto chair of the one-person Historical and Theological Studies Department at Unity Institute, located at Unity Village, Missouri. His Q&A column, "That's a Good Question," has been one of the most popular features in *Unity Magazine* since the 1990s. Dr. Shepherd is the author of three books on theology, church history and practical spirituality: *Glimpses of Truth* (UFBL Press, 2000), *Friends in High Places* (iUniverse, 2006, 3rd edition), and *Good Questions* (Unity House, 2009); he also writes science fiction novels under the pen name *Thomas Henry Quell.*

While living in California, Shepherd produced and moderated the critically acclaimed local access TV program *Coffee with the Clergy,* a twice-weekly interfaith panel discussion, featuring interaction among religious leaders from diverse backgrounds on a wide range of topics which usually explored areas that were frankly controversial.

Currently teaching at Unity Institute, Dr. Shepherd finds time to host *Let's Talk About It*, a weekly Internet radio program on Unity.FM, and is "plodding through" several book-length writing projects. Dr. Tom, as his students call him, has ordained ministerial standing with Unity Worldwide Ministries (formerly the Association of Unity Churches International), the Unitarian Universalist Association, and the National Association of Congregational Christian Churches. He lives in Lee's Summit, Missouri, with his wife Carol-Jean.

Dr. Shepherd's website is *www.metaphysicaltheology.com* and his Theo-Blog can be found at *http://revtom-theo-blog.blogspot.com/*.

Printed in the U.S.A.

B0022